White Girls in Moccasins

White Girls in Moccasins

Yolanda Bonnell

SCIROCCO DRAMA

White Girls in Moccasins
first published 2023 by Scirocco Drama
An imprint of J. Gordon Shillingford Publishing Inc.
© 2023 Yolanda Bonnell

Scirocco Drama Editor: Glenda MacFarlane
Cover design by Doowah Design
Trout Dream cover images by Rihkee Strapp
Author photo by Bliss Thompson
Production photos by Dahlia Katz and Jeremy Mimnagh

Printed and bound in Canada on 100% post-consumer recycled paper.
We acknowledge the financial support of the Manitoba Arts Council and
The Canada Council for the Arts for our publishing program.

Production inquiries to:
yolanda@manidoons.com

Anishinaabemowin translations by Lena Recollet and Sally Atchitawens-Recollet

*The Playwright acknowledges the assistance of the 2018 Banff Playwrights Lab—
a partnership between the Banff Centre for Arts and Creativity and
the Canada Council for the Arts.*

White Girls in Moccasins *was created on the land of Tkarón:to where the original
caretakers include the Mississaugas of the Credit River, as well as other Anishinaabe
peoples, the Haudenosaunee-Six Nations Confederacy and the Wendat.
It was also created in Minhrpa—Treaty 7 territory—the traditional
lands of the Stoney Nakoda, The Blackfoot and the Tsuut'ina.*

Library and Archives Canada Cataloguing in Publication

Title: White girls in moccasins / Yolanda Bonnell.
Names: Bonnell, Yolanda, 1982- author.
Identifiers: Canadiana 20220492867 | ISBN 9781990738241 (softcover)
Classification: LCC PS8603.O575 W55 2023 | DDC C812/.6—dc23

J. Gordon Shillingford Publishing
P.O. Box 86, RPO Corydon Avenue, Winnipeg, MB Canada R3M 3S3

Dedicated to my brown siblings and any Indigenous kin who might feel lost.

Yolanda Bonnell

Yolanda Bonnell *(She/They)* is a Bi/Queer 2 Spirit Anishinaabe-Ojibwe, South Asian mixed performer, playwright and multidisciplinary creator/facilitator. From Fort William First Nation in Thunder Bay, Ontario *(Superior Robinson Treaty territory)*, her arts practice is now based in Tkarón:to. In February 2020, Yolanda's four-time Dora-nominated solo show *bug* was remounted at Theatre Passe Muraille, while the published book was shortlisted for a Governor General's Literary Award. In 2022, her play *White Girls in Moccasins* was produced at Buddies in Bad Times Theatre in Tkarón:to and the frank theatre on Coast Salish Territory. Yolanda was the first Indigenous artist recipient of the Jayu Arts for Human Rights Award for her work and won the PGC Tom Hendry Drama Award for her play *My Sister's Rage*. Yolanda has facilitated workshops at schools, including York University and Sheridan College, and she proudly bases her practice in land-based creation, drawing on energy and inspiration from the earth and her ancestors.

Acknowledgements
~ Gitchi miigwetch ~

My deepest gratitude to Clare Preuss for all of the guidance and seed planting for the container of this story.

To Binaeshee Quae for bringing the spirit and voice of Ziibi off of the page while I was creating.

Elizabeth Staples—my white-winged dove muse—for being so in sync with me.

The sweet Ravyn Wngz for embodying my ancestral river so gorgeously.

To Cole Alvis, for seeing me and always understanding my brain.

And Samantha Brown for breathing such beautiful life and fullness into Miskozi, so I could see her fully.

Miigwetch also to Mary Bonnell, Nathenia Bonnell, Sam Bonnell, Bilal Baig, Isaac Thomas, Keith Barker, Native Earth Performing Arts, Zita Nyarady, Cathy Elliot, Sarah Gartshore, Diana Belshaw, Mel Hague, Evalyn Parry, Buddies in Bad Times Theatre, Jessica Lea Fleming, Ashley Bomberry, Miali Buscemi, fu-GEN Theatre, Brian Quirt, Jenna Rodgers, Amanda Cordner, Emilie Leclerc, Quelemia Sparrow, Kristen Padayas, Michaela Washburn, Kat MacLean, Mirae Lee, Charissa Wilcox, Lisa Alves, Indrit Kasapi, lemonTree Creations Studio, Aqua Nibii Waawaaskone, Aria Evans, Brefny Caribou, Theresa Cutknife, Sheila Demerah, Mary Magiskan, Jason Goudreau, Nikki Shaffeullah, Michelle Lynne Soicher, Donna-Michelle

St. Bernard, Tanisha Taitt, Alison Wong, Natasha Parsons, Tarragon Theatre, Wildseed Centre for Art and Activism, Kay Chan, Ty Sloane, 2 Spirit of the First Nations, Daniel Carter, Lena Recollet, Sally Atchitawens-Recollet, Roger Roulette, Natércia Napoleão, Steph Raposo, Aidan Morishita-Miki, Dylan Tate-Howarth, Maddie Bautista, Echo Zhou, Rachel Forbes, Rihkee Strapp, Trevor Schwellnus, Sruthi Suresan, Asli Ozuak, Rebecca Vandevelde, Samira Banihashemi, Sebastian Marziali, Jonathan MacArthur, Ada Aguilar, Jac Costa, Dylan Mitro, Vanessa Magic, Robert Weir, Anais West, Fay Nass, the frank theatre, Danica Charlie, Lisa C. Ravensbergen, Emily Jane King, Jay Havens, Mary Jane Coomber, Lauchlin Johnston, Candelario Andrade, Andrew Pye, Jessica Adamson, Ivy Charles, Debbie Courchene, Talking Stick Festival, Full Circle: First Nations Performance, Amy Ireland, Courage Bacchus, Monica Garrido and Pauline Shirt.

Playwright's Notes

White Girls in Moccasins is not my story. It belongs to so many of us.

I have a habit of weaving bits of myself, my truths, my realities and experiences into my stories. But my contribution is only a part of the whole.

It is definitely a rough sketch of my identity journey. I grew up on and off my reservation, never understanding the history and truth of what it meant to be Ojibwe in so-called Canada. And what you may not know is that every reservation—every community—is different and has a different relationship to cultural reclamation. Some were able to retain language and medicine teachings, for example, others were not.

When I was first writing this story, I had a conversation with my Auntie Milly. I was (re)introducing her to smudging and she admitted to me that she felt like a fraud when partaking in the medicine. It broke my heart, but I fully related and told her that it was even a line in the play. We grew up very Catholic—the church had a firm grip, so the integration of traditional practices can be difficult for some of our elders. It was wild to me that so many of us felt this way. That despite growing up clearly Indigenous, that we didn't feel like we deserved ceremony, that we didn't have access to it, that Ojibwe culture was not ours to experience.

My auntie very sadly passed away in 2020, so I can only hope that I can begin to try and heal her and my other ancestors through these types of stories. Where I call them in. Where we welcome them to ceremony. And show them that these medicines and experiences have always been theirs.

I wrote this story for all of us who feel whitewashed and are fumbling through reclamation. A reminder that you are just as Indigenous whether you are able and ready or even want to engage in culturally specific ways of living or not.

I also want to give a deep, special acknowledgement to Samantha Brown, who embodied Miskozi for so long while I shaped the story. Sam brought more than just herself to the role and there aren't enough words for how grateful I am for her voice and contribution to the growth of it.

This story—these stories are as much hers as they are mine as they are yours. And as the colonial apocalypse continues to rage on around us, inside of us, everywhere—I have to keep remembering the importance of storytelling within the revolution; uplifting our communities by letting them know that they are not alone. I hope you find that in this story.

Foreword
By Donna-Michelle St. Bernard

On the way home from *White Girls in Moccasins* I turned to the director, Cole Alvis, and remarked, "That was a lot of whiteness."
Cole replied drily, "Donna, it's literally in the title."
It is there. It's everywhere. That's kind of the point.

"our indigenous bodies have been the site for the colonizers' gaze, the site where the West was won and conquered over and over again."[1]

Whiteness is...
Constant
Ever-present
Assumed
Expected
Modelled

Whiteness is ...
Normal
Natural
Neutral
Common
Standard
Classic

We are...
Immersed
Acclimatized

---

[1] Michelle Olson, *Performing Indigeneity*, Playwrights Canada Press.

Indoctrinated
Swaddled
Steeped
    ... in whiteness.

But inside, under, alongside and through all of that, this play is underscored by thrumming insistence, naming the other immersions, constancies, presences that pervade life on Turtle Island. Some of these are inventoried in Ziibi's hasty packing upon threat of contact:
baskets for the museums,
sage for the white witches,
dream catchers for the wellness retreats.

Indigeneity is ineradicable, with the inevitability suggested by Octavia Butler,
"all that you touch
You change.
All that you change
Changes you."[2]

Generations later we find our contemporary protagonist, Miskozi, at sea in self-judgment and recrimination, awash in the brine of Vanna White, Jordan Knight and Stevie Nicks. And it is with these elements that the play offers us frybread, ribbon skirts: a repurposing of what is needed from what is made available, however nutrient-devoid or tacky. Reclamation is active, intentional. Miskozi pilots this journey, responsive to Ziibi's prompting and coloured by Waabishkizi's constant companionship. Surreal shapeshifting pulls us along a route of unsettledness no less disorienting than the theft and displacement that premises this journey. Under Ziibi's mischievous guidance, things shift often—who and what we are seeing, who and what we think we are.

---

[2] Octavia Butler, *Parable of the Sower*, Grand Central Publishing.

This play is grounded in the tension of a duality, an inescapable simultaneity where in each of us is what Miskozi calls *"a room, within a room, within a room."*

Bonnell's play lets us know early on to look for what is hidden, to recognize what has always been there. It secretes vital knowledge in jokes and jabs at soft places. It breathes in bodies where it is not recognized. It hides in plain sight—that is how this knowledge persists. As you experience this play, you would do well to avail yourself of all your senses, not just the usual eight. You would be well advised to keep three eyes open: this space is alive with secrets, codes and clues.

"there's so many stories we have kept secret... and once you tell the story, it's a freedom!"[3]

We are invited to take things which have been made uncommon and become re-familiar.

Crack yourself all the way open and don't expect to catch it all. Audiences of the premiere production found themselves encircled by projected animation deepening the experience and the room vibrated with access measures, ceremony, medicine, music and dance that, too, carried story/ knowledge to us, if we could see, accept, embrace, interpret— each of us meeting the piece as we are equipped/ receptive.

"does it matter that the audience does not apprehend the ceremony that the artists have created and woven into the fabric of the performance?"[4]

The body is the site of constant scrutiny/criticism. Despite that, so much appears to be taken, hidden, obscured. Yet much of what remains is in the body, at times indistinguishable from instinct or habit. Still, the body remembers, *"knead, knead, pat, roll, cut, cut, cut."*

---

[3]   Muriel Miguel, interview with Jo Reed, November 16, 2018, National Endowment for the Arts.
[4]   Yvette Nolan, *Medicine Shows: Indigenous Performance Culture*, Playwrights Canada Press.

There are white girls in the title, and in the moccasins. But what has always been here is
Patient,
Persistent,
Foundational,
Real.
Real.

January 2023

Donna-Michelle St. Bernard (a.k.a. Belladonna the Blest) is an emcee, playwright, and agitator. DM is the creator of the 54ology and artistic director of New Harlem Productions.

Production History

White Girls in Moccasins began development as part of the Animikiig Creator's Unit at Native Earth Performing Arts between 2016 and 2017 with an excerpt performed at the Weesageechak Begins to Dance Festival. Clare Preuss was brought on as dramaturg and director and the cast was Yolanda Bonnell (*Miskozi*) and Zita Nyarady (*Waabishkizi*).

It was further developed to have a four-day run at the 39th Rhubarb Festival at Buddies in Bad Times Theatre, where the cast included Yolanda Bonnell (*Miskozi*), Elizabeth Staples (*Waabishkizi*) as well as Binaeshee Quae (*Ziibi*) as a third character was added. Clare Preuss stayed on as dramaturg and director as the play moved into development at the Banff Playwrights Lab in April of 2018.

An excerpt of the show was then performed at the 2 Spirit Cabaret (*Buddies in Bad Times Theatre, Native Earth Performing Arts)* with Samantha Brown (*Miskozi*), Kat MacLean (*Waabishkizi*) and Yolanda Bonnell (*Ziibi*) in the cast. Yolanda was then brought on as playwright-in-residence at Buddies with the piece.

In 2019, a two-week workshop and public reading at Buddies in Bad Times was produced and supported by Yolanda and manidoons collective with Samantha Brown (*Miskozi*), Elizabeth Staples (*Waabishkizi*) and Brefny Caribou (*Ziibi*) as cast with Yolanda directing. manidoons collective then became a part of the Buddies' residency program to prepare the show for production in 2021.

The production was pushed to 2022 due to the COVID-19 pandemic. An online workshop with Samantha Brown (*Miskozi*), Elizabeth Staples (*Waabishkizi*) and Binaeshee Quae

(*Ziibi*) was completed before heading into a rehearsal workshop for production later that year.

In February 2022, *White Girls in Moccasins* had its world premiere at Buddies in Bad Times Theatre in partnership with manidoons collective, followed by a digital run.

Creative Team

Yolanda Bonnell...Miskozi

Elizabeth Staples ....Waabishkizi

Ravyn Wngz...Ziibi

Directed by Cole Alvis and Samantha Brown

Trevor Schwellnus...............................Set and Projection Design

Rihkee Strapp...............Animation and Associate Video Design

Echo Zhou ....Lighting Design

Sruthi Suresan....................................Associate Lighting Design

Maddie Bautista ....Composer and Sound design

Rachel Forbes..Costume Design

Asli Ozuak... Associate Costume Design, Set and Props Coordinator

Natércia Napoleão .... Associate Producer

Dylan Tate-Howarth...Stage Manager

Ada Aguilar ....Rehearsal Stage Manager

Show Regalia:

      Moccasins created by: Sheila Demerah

      Belt created by: Mary Magiskan

      Drum created by: Aqua Nibii Waawaaskone

      Drum painted by: Nathenia Bonnell and Sam Bonnell

      Gramma's hands inspiration: Mary Bonnell

Lena Recollet, Sally Atchitawens-Recollet and Roger Roulette ....Anishinaabemowin language keepers

Pauline Shirt ....Knowledge keeper

Amy Ireland and Courage Bacchu .... Deaf interpreters

In June 2022, *White Girls in Moccasins* was produced at the frank theatre (Coast Salish Territory), co-presented by the Talking Stick Festival & Full Circle: First Nations Performance.

Creative Team

Danica Charlie .... Miskozi

Emily Jane King .... Waabishkizi

Lisa C. Ravensbergen .... Ziibi

Directed by Quelemia Sparrow

Mary Jane Coomber .... Sound Design

Lauchlin Johnston .... Set Design

Jay Havens .... Costumes Design

Candelario Andrade .... Projection Design

Andrew Pye .... Lighting Design

Jay Havens ..... Animation Content Creation & Poster Artwork

Jessica Adamson .... Stage Management

Ivy Charles .... Assistant Stage Management

Debbie Courchene .... Production Management

Anais West & Fay Nass .... Co-producers

Marguerite Witvoet .... Music Consultant and Vocal Coach

Katie Voravong .... Intimacy Consultant

Lisa C. Ravensbergen .... Creative and Cultural Consultant

Funding support from the Toronto Arts Council, Ontario Arts Council RGTC: Nightwood Theatre, Buddies in Bad Times Theatre, Studio 180, fu-GEN Theatre, Native Earth Performing Arts.

Ziibi (Binaeshee Quae) sings "There's nothing more dangerous than a white woman" with Miskozi (Yolanda Bonnell) in the back. Rhubarb Festival, 2018. Photo by Dahlia Katz.

Alabaster Baby. "My first relationship was with a white woman. We were teenagers." Miskozi (Yolanda Bonnell) and Waabishkizi (Elizabeth Staples). Rhubarb Festival, 2018. Photo by Dahlia Katz.

Waabishkizi (Elizabeth Staples) watches as Miskozi (Yolanda Bonnell) addresses the studio audience. Rhubarb Festival, 2018. Photo by Dahlia Katz.

"There's a place where healing begins." Ziibi (Binaeshee Quae), Miskozi (Yolanda Bonnell) and Waabishkizi (Elizabeth Staples) begin to heal. Rhubarb Festival, 2018. Photo by Dahlia Katz.

Ziibi (Ravyn Wngz) and Little Nish Child (Yolanda Bonnell) try to hold on during the cyclone of colonization. Buddies in Bad Times production. Photo by Jeremy Mimnagh.

"Step by Step!" Ziibi (Ravyn Wngz), Miskozi (Yolanda Bonnell) and Waabishkizi (Elizabeth Staples) become the boy band, New Kids on the Block. Buddies in Bad Times production. Photo by Jeremy Mimnagh.

"I danced around my coffee table pretending I was at their concert!" Ziibi (Ravyn Wngz) and Waabishkizi (Elizabeth Staples) sing "I'll Be Loving You Forever." Buddies in Bad Times production. Photo by Jeremy Mimnagh.

Miskozi (Yolanda Bonnell) sits in front of the Wheel of Privilege board, with her ancestors watching. Buddies in Bad Times production. Photo by Jeremy Mimnagh.

Ziibi (Ravyn Wngz) tries to make Miskozi remember where she comes from. Buddies in Bad Times production. Photo by Jeremy Mimnagh.

Miskozi (Yolanda Bonnell) submerged in the blizzard. Buddies in Bad Times production. Photo by Jeremy Mimnagh.

Characters

MISKOZI (Mis-koh-zih) She is red:
An Anishinaabe femme. (The actor who plays Miskozi also plays LITTLE NISH CHILD.)

WAABISHKIZI (Waa-bish-kih-zih) She is white:
A white femme, specifically, Miskozi's inner white girl. (The actor who plays Waabishkizi also plays many others.)

ZIIBI (Zee-bih) Ancestral river:
An Anishinaabe femme, an ancestor, hand drummer* and singer. (The actor who plays Ziibi also plays many others.)

*The performer does not need to hand drum, a track can be used.

Song List

THERE IS A PLACE
Ziibi

REMEMBER (BIINJIIY'II GI-MSKWII-M)
Ziibi

NIDEHEM
Ziibi

THERE'S NOTHING MORE DANGEROUS
Ziibi

PILLS & PINS
Mizkozi and Waabishkizi

THE NUMBING
All

REMEMBER (BIINJIIY'II GI-MSKWII-M) (reprise)
Ziibi and ancestor voices

THERE IS A PLACE (reprise)
Ziibi and Miskozi

Setting

There is no traditional setting for this story. It takes place in the past, in the now and is only somewhat linear. The convention being that when Miskozi was tasked with "finding something" and "looking back to go forward," she time hops all the way back not only to her own beginnings where the actual seed of feeling whitewashed was planted, but to where it all began: first contact.

So—if we're being technical—the base setting is the In-Between Place, which is actually the sweat lodge. But within that there are many other settings that are created to support Miskozi's memories, dreams and visions like her house on the rez, a school playground, her grandmother's kitchen, the living room, a Greyhound and various studios that host the most surreal and strange ancestral game show.

Notes on Text

A forward slash / indicates an overlap in dialogue.

Text in CAPS is sung.

Text in open brackets ( ) indicates the phonetics of the Anishinaabemowin and then the English translation

Production Notes

SOMETHING GROWING: The stage direction of "something grows" is represented as the choice—or the imposition—of ingesting white supremacy and colonialism, and is to be interpreted physically however the director(s) and designers choose.

The singular word stage directions are to help evoke the sense or energy of those moments. Or what those moments might need: *confusion, breath, love ...*

BODY: This story is meant to be told with movement—whatever that means to you. There are moments indicated where movement scores are an integral part of the scene. But feel free to choose other moments to move or dance to, or you can also choose stillness.

SONG: The songs in the script do have a melody to them. You are free to come up with your own or to contact the author to inquire about recordings.

LANGUAGE: Anishinaabemowin has many different dialects from all over. If you are a speaker/language keeper and your dialect is different from what's written in the script, you can absolutely use your own dialect for Ziibi's words and sentences instead.

PROTOCOL: Please smudge the space before and after each sharing, leave out a spirit chair for the ancestors, and find ways of caring for yourselves in the work.

The following poem was written sort of as a companion piece to this story. For our production, we recorded it and had both the English and Anishinaabemowin versions playing to set the tone as witnesses walked in. It can be used or not used.

A Cycle

Like a helium balloon someone let go of me one day
I float
Out in space feeling as if there is nothing I can grab a hold of
Air
Just air
And my eyes are closed — sometimes sewn shut
Sometimes I hold them shut tightly for I have a fear of heights
There is not knowing
Not understanding
Not feeling ... complete
Completeness
Lost
Yes
I am lost
In this space that refuses to hold me
In the hands that refuse to hold on to me
Spinning
I try so many different ways of floating
Of trying to work with this toxic gravity
Trying to make myself look like a cloud
I puff myself up
Yet somehow remain small
I am a cloud
I am a cloud
I am a cloud
I proclaim it deep within myself
Hoping
That it will make me feel right
Hoping
That it will make me feel
Complete
Completeness

But I am not a cloud
And if I am not a cloud
Then what am I?
A ghost?
A spirit?
A balloon?
Question after question
Questioning after questioning
I realize
That I can't find answers with my eyes shut

So I decide to open them
I open
And I look down at my feet
And they are
Planted
Deep
Within the earth
I am rooted
And the roots spread so far and so deep and connect with other roots
And the waters
I open
I am bigger than the clouds
I am not a ghost or a spirit or a balloon
I am an ancestor
I am wind
I am elemental voices rising in the cold night air
I am the earth
The trees hold onto me
I hold on to myself
I hold on
Hold on

A Cycle
(Translated into Anishinaabemowin by Roger Roulette)

*Daabishkoo giitwaamiseg bagidinaman gaa-bimaasing, mii
ningoding gaa-izhiseyaan.*
Bimaasing
Daabishkoo giizhiganaadong, gaawiin gegoo ji-debibidoowan.
Noodin
Noodin eta
Nimbazangwaab - giboogwaadegin
*Naanigoding nimbazangwaab ningotaan aaniish ishpiming ji-
zegi'igoowaan*
Gaawiin ji-gikendaagosinog
Nisidotanziwaan
Moozhitoosiwaan...giizhiseg
Giizhisewin
Wanishin
Eya
Niwanishin
Giizhigaanaadong ji-minjiminisog
Oninjiing ji-minjiminisinog
Gizhibaaseg
Nanaandok nindoodam ji-bimaashiyaan
Ji-wiijitoowaan akiing epinigoowaan
Daabishkoo aanakwad ji-izhinaagoziyaan
Nimangi'idiz
Giiyaabi dash nindagaashiiw
Nindaanakwadiw
Nindaanakwadiw
Nindaanakwadiw
Mii enindizowaan
Bagosendamaan
Ji-minwendamaambaan
Bagosendamaan
Ji-nayendamaan
Giizhiseg
Giizhisewin
Gaawiin dash nindaanakwadiwisii
Nindaanakwadiwisiwaan
Aweneniwiyaan?

Jiibay?
Jiibekaan?
Gaa-bimaasing?
Ayani-gagwedwewin
Ishkwaa aanike-gagwedwewinan
Nimaamikaw
Nimbwaanawitoon ji-nakwetamaan bazangwaabiyaan
Nandawaa nimbaakinaanan
Nimbaakinaan
Ninzidan ninganawaabandaanan
Mii dash
Ashidakiiwan
Anaaming
Akiing
Nindoojiibikow
Zaswegigin anaaming ojiibikong izhi
Nibiing gaye
Mii nawach mindidowaan apiich aanakwadoon
Gaawiin ninjiibewisii, jiibekaanisii gemaa bemaasiinziwaan
Nindaanikoodaaganiw
Ninoondiniw
Ninoondaagoz izhi dibikaag ezhi-dakaasing
Nindakiw
Mitigoog ninagaanigoog
Niminjiminidiz
Niminjimaakwii
Niminjiminige

Prologue: River of Stars

Stars.

We hear the voice of a river manifested.
In moonlight,
ZIIBI is weaving;
ZIIBI is singing,
As she always has been and continues to do
Ever present.

As she weaves, the world grows around her.
She expands.
The riverbank expands.
Her voice echoes.

There Is a Place

ZIIBI:

WEY YA HEY YAA WEY HEY YA WEY YA AH
WEY YA HEY YAA WEY HEY YA WEY YA

WEY YA HEY YAA WEY HEY YA WEY YA AH
WEY YA HEY YAA WEY HEY YA WEY YA

A LITTLE NISH CHILD comes out, in
moccasins.
She begins to weave and sing with ZIIBI;
the pace picks up.
They mirror each other, playing.

ZIIBI & LITTLE
NISH CHILD: WEY YA HEY YAA WEY HEY YA WEY YA AH
WEY YA HEY YAA WEY HEY YA WEY YA

WEY YA HEY YAA WEY HEY YA WEY YA AH
WEY YA HEY YAA WEY HEY YA WEY YA

They stare at each other.

Breath.

*ZIIBI steps out of the river to her human
form and stands next to the LITTLE NISH
CHILD.*
They both stare at their reflections.

LITTLE NISH
CHILD:

Through my waterways
Slipping down the tide
Of my blood
The trout fish lives in my bones

ZIIBI sings to her.
*As she sings, she teaches the LITTLE NISH
CHILD how to gather wild rice.*

They gather together.

ZIIBI:

THERE IS A PLACE WHERE GRASS USED
TO GROW
WHERE STONES WHISPERED TO ME IN
MY DREAMS
LIKE THE WIND, LIKE WATER RIPPLING
THERE IS A PLACE MY MOTHER HELD
ME
AND WOULD SING STORIES OF STARS
AND WOULD SING STORIES OF STARS
THERE IS A PLACE LONG AGO
WHERE ANCESTORS SAY WE'RE NEVER
ALONE

Biinjiiy'ii gi-mskwii-m
(been-jee-yuh-ee gih-miss-gwee'm)   *inside your blood*
Nji-aki-ing maajiishka
(Njih akih-ing ma-jeesh-guh)   *from the earth*
Gi-Kaawiikaa gwiinaw

(Gih-gaa-wee-gaa gween-awey)   *you're never lost/*
uncertain/restless

Hmm?

You are never lost

> *LITTLE NISH CHILD nods.*
> *ZIIBI kisses the top of her head.*
>
> *Thunder/Animikiig.*
> *A bolt of lightning.*

ZIIBI: Ooh, looks like a storm is moving in. Come.
We should head back.

> *The opening drums from "God Save the*
> *Queen" are heard.*
> *The two turn around ominously and*
> *slightly confused.*
>
> *Beat.*

LITTLE NISH
CHILD: What /

> *She is cut off by the trumpet in the song*
> *continuing with a mix of the* Jaws *theme or*
> *something else that is foreboding.*
>
> *They feel a rumble in the earth.*
> *In their bodies.*
> *Something approaches.*
>
> *The wind begins to stir.*

LITTLE NISH
CHILD: What's happening?

ZIIBI: I don't know.

LITTLE NISH
CHILD: Do you feel that?
Where is it coming from??

ZIIBI: We should go now.

                    She is cut off by the lyrics of the song
                    coming in:

                    "God save our gracious Queen
                    Long live our noble Queen…"

                    The two look at each other and scream.
                    The song continues.

                    They break into a panic while the song
                    plays, running around, gathering and
                    yelling the following lines.
                    (They are not actually gathering physical
                    items.)

                    First contact.

ZIIBI: Go! Go! Go! Grab what you can!

LITTLE NISH
CHILD: Should we take canoe??

ZIIBI: Get wild rice!

LITTLE NISH
CHILD: I got jingle dresses!
                    Where did we put language??

ZIIBI: I–I don't know! I was just using it!

LITTLE NISH
CHILD: I have a–a–a braid? Where is the / other

ZIIBI: / Bury the ceremonies in that corner!

                    LNC buries the ceremonies.

LITTLE NISH
CHILD: What do I do with these land teachings??

ZIIBI: Toss 'em! I'll bury them over here!

LITTLE NISH
CHILD: Ahh, they're getting closer! Should I take
                  these birchbark / bask—

ZIIBI: / No! No! Leave baskets—they'll need them
                  for the museums!

LITTLE NISH
CHILD: The what!?

ZIIBI: It doesn't matter!
                  What medicines do you have?!

LITTLE NISH
CHILD: I mean—I have... sweetgrass...uhh, there's
                  some sage!

ZIIBI: No! No! The white witches will need the sage!

LITTLE NISH
CHILD: I'm taking it anyways!

ZIIBI: Some seeds!

> *ZIIBI tosses an invisible bag of seeds to
> LNC.*

LITTLE NISH
CHILD: Sh–should I take dreamcatchers!?

ZIIBI: If you take dreamcatchers, what will they
                  craft at their wellness retreats!??!

LITTLE NISH
CHILD: I'm *sorry*!! I'm *panicking*!!
                  And I can't find second braid!

ZIIBI: Well—we'll just have to do with the one then.
                  Or or or—I don't know—cut our hair!

> *They both gasp dramatically.*
> *ZIIBI covers her mouth.*
> *LITTLE NISH CHILD grabs her own hair.*

ZIIBI: I'm sorry.
I didn't mean it.

> *The wind suddenly picks up and blows harder,*
> *and they are caught up in*
> *the cyclone from* The Wizard of Oz —
> *AKA the Cyclone of Colonization*
> *(whatever that looks like to you).*
> *There is faint drumming.*
> *The fur trade.*
> *Bibles and rosaries whip by.*
> *King George III flies by on a broomstick.*
> *He changes into a laughing John A. Macdonald:*
> *"Kill the Indian in the child!"*
> *He disappears.*
> *Hudson's Bay blankets fly by.*
>
> *Remnants of colonial items fall into the river.*
> *The river picks them up.*
>
> *The cyclone continues with:*
> *The crying Indian*
> *Chief Wahoo*
> *The Indian Act*
> *Land-O-Lakes Butter*
> *The White Paper.*
>
> *The river is dammed up.*
>
> *It is a storm of epic proportions.*
> *Time and space shift.*
>
> *WAABISHKIZI and MISKOZI get spit out of the storm in the distant future.*

Birth

The In-Between Place.
Smoke.
Embers.
Sparks.

LITTLE NISH CHILD has become
MISKOZI.
Her moccasins are gone.
ZIIBI is gone.
WAABISHKIZI stands behind her, looking
around.
MISKOZI doesn't know she's there.

Something germinates.

MISKOZI stands, braced, with her eyes
closed, holding on to the "things" her
ancestor gathered.
She is out of breath.

She opens her eyes and sees the witnesses
for the first time.
Confused, she slowly places the things in
the corner.
When she puts them down, the sound of the
bells on the jingle dress rattle.
She moves the "pile" away with her foot;
they jingle again.

MISKOZI inspects the witnesses.
WAABISHKIZI moves behind her, sort of
mimicking her movements.
MISKOZI leans into a witness; she's about
to boop their nose, when WAABISHKIZI
pops her head down next to her to inspect
the witness in the next seat.
MISKOZI jumps, startled.

MISKOZI: Ahh! *(Or some form of exclamation: "Jesus!"*
                   "Tha fuck?!")

                           The two study each other.

MISKOZI: Who / are you?

WAABISHKIZI: / Who are you?

MISKOZI: Where did / you come from?

WAABISHKIZI: / Where did you come from?

MISKOZI: Who / put you here?

WAABISHKIZI: / Who put you here?

MISKOZI: Okay, stop!
                   (Beat.)
                   Who are you?

WAABISHKIZI: I'm you.

MISKOZI: What?

WAABISHKIZI: I'm YOU.

MISKOZI: N–no, you're not.

WAABISHKIZI: Yes, I am.

MISKOZI: No, you're–you're obviously not...

WAABISHKIZI: Well, okay... I guess I'm—yes, I am a *part* of
                   you.

MISKOZI: Which part?

WAABISHKIZI: Well, see—you're... you're what they call—a
                   coconut.

MISKOZI: A–a coconut?

WAABISHKIZI: Oh, I'm sorry. A potato.

MISKOZI: Did you just call me a potato?

WAABISHKIZI: An apple?

MISKOZI: What?

WAABISHKIZI: A turnip?
No—that can't be right.
A rutabaga?
What's the difference between a rutabaga and a turnip? Are they the same thing?

> *Disbelief.*

MISKOZI: I'm dead, right?
This is being dead.
Did a streetcar finally get me?!

WAABISHKIZI: Nope.
We're inside—

> *She touches MISKOZI's stomach and heart.*
> *Beat.*
> *Then she boops her nose and says "Boop."*

> *Confusion.*

WAABISHKIZI: But I don't know how we got here.
Tell me how we got here.
(Beat.)
What's wrong?

> *MISKOZI begins to repeat a lost movement slowly.*

MISKOZI: I—
I feel like I've lost something and I don't know what it is.
There's something… missing?

WAABISHKIZI: Tell me.

MISKOZI: I don't know what it is, but I know I've lost something.

WAABISHKIZI: Where did it begin?

MISKOZI: And I'm scared.

WAABISHKIZI: Tell me.

MISKOZI: And my feet are cold.

> *A dam cracks.*
> *A sudden rush of water.*
> *Large and loud.*
> *It submerges everything and surrounds them.*
>
> *Breath.*
>
> *ZIIBI flows out.*
>
> *The two girls don't notice ZIIBI, but they feel her presence the way ancestors make their presence known in our daily lives—like when a picture falls out of nowhere. Maybe something falls or rolls across the floor.*

ZIIBI: White fur.
              Brown-skinned.
              Flowered dress.

MISKOZI: What was that?

WAABISHKIZI: Mmm, the wind?

ZIIBI: Are you for real right now?

MISKOZI: Yeah, maybe.
              I mean—does wind even exist... here?

ZIIBI: Ho-leh—bigger arrival than grand entry and nothin' from these two!?

WAABISHKIZI: Tell me how it began.

MISKOZI: How it...?

Oh... okay. I—well, I was born in a small house.

Transition into The Living Room.

Smaller than this room!
It could fit in the palm of my grandpa's hand.
And it did.
It did.

MISKOZI and WAABISHKIZI begin a movement sequence, building a home base.

MISKOZI: A room, within a room, within a room
Soft and warm.
Like a womb.
Like the moccasins my grandpa made for me.

MISKOZI &
WAABISHKIZI: It enveloped me.

MISKOZI: Kept me safe.
Secure.
And loved.
I would sit against his thumb as he told me stories and stroked my hair.

MISKOZI &
WAABISHKIZI: My hair!

MISKOZI: Long and dark

WAABISHKIZI: It grew forever.

MISKOZI: I wanted it to grow forever
My hair made me feel beautiful.
My gramma had long hair.
Salt and pepper buns.

MISKOZI &
WAABISHKIZI: My gramma...

MISKOZI: This house.
                  Had one kitchen with a big freezer—for all
                  of the moose meat. One toilet but no bathtub.
                  One bedroom with one bed. And one living
                  room with one fireplace and one small
                  television set.
                  And like 50 fly traps hanging from the ceiling.
                  Six of us lived here.

Remember (Biinjiiy'ii Gi-Mskwii-M)

                  ZIIBI begins to beat a hand drum.

                  *She sings a song to try and remind
                  MISKOZI where she comes from and who
                  she is.*

                  *Movement sequence while she sings.
                  MISKOZI and WAABISHKIZI mimicking
                  and exploring each other.
                  Never noticing ZIIBI.*

                  *During the last verse of the song, MISKOZI
                  and WAABISHKIZI stop and stare forward
                  as if they're watching television, ignoring
                  ZIIBI.*

ZIIBI: BIINJIIY'II GI
                  (been-jee-yuh-ee gih)   *inside your blood*
                  BIINJIIY'II GI
                  BIINJIIY'II GI
                  MSKWII-M
                  (miss-gwee'm)
                  BIINJIIY'II GI
                  BIINJIIY'II GI
                  BIINJIIY'II GI
                  MSKWII-M
                  GI-KAÀWIIKAA

(Gih-gaa-wee-gaa)   *You are never lost*
GI-KAAWIIKAA
GI-KAAWIIKAA
GWIINAW WAY HEY YO
(gweenaw)
GI-KAAWIIKAA
GI-KAAWIIKAA
GI-KAAWIIKAA
GWIINAW WAY HEY YO

(Repeat.)

GWIINAW WAY HEY YO
GWIINAW WAY HEY YO
GWIINAW WAY HEY YO

> *ZIIBI beats the drum once.*
> *Hard.*
> *Loud.*

> *The two pay no attention.*
> *ZIIBI looks at them.*
> *Looks to the "TV."*
> *Looks back at them.*
> *She tries to get MISKOZI's attention like*
> *an angry auntie.*

ZIIBI: Hey!
Nishke!   **(Nishkay)**   *Look!*
Nishke!   **(Nishkay)**
Gshkozi.   **(Shkozih)**   *Open your eyes*
Miskozi, Gshkozi!

> *Sigh.*

Okay.

> *She sets down the drum.*
> *Decides to try a different approach…*

The Game

Transition into Studio 1.

ZIIBI: (*As TV announcer.*) Froooom Hollywood, it's
              America's game!
              A show the whole family can enjoy!
              Filled with fun! Glamour! Excitement!
              Surprises!
              It's—

              Everyone!

ALL: Wheel!!
              Of!!
              Privilege!!

              Wheel of Fortune *theme song, in vocables.*
              (Can be vocalized by ZIIBI and WAABISH-
              KIZI.)

              Excitement.

              Projection: "Applause"
              The audience cheers.

              WAABISHKIZI becomes Vanna White and
              ZIIBI becomes Pat Sajak.

              Projection: A Wheel of Fortune *game*
              board.

              Look here and smile.

MISKOZI: This is the first television show I ever
              remember watching.

MISKOZI spins the wheel.

Projection: "Applause"
The audience cheers.

MISKOZI: "T" please!

ZIIBI: *(As Pat Sajak.)* One "T"!

Projection: "Applause"
The audience cheers.

WAABISHKI does a movement and turns one "T."

MISKOZI: There was always a "T."
(Beat.)
She was the first idea of what true beauty meant to me.
Blonde.
Slim.
Pretty.
Her last name was White, for Godsakes.
I wanted to be like her.
Admired and desired.
You could see the universe in Vanna's smile.
She was on the cover of all the magazines.
Always with that smile.
And those dresses!
I wondered what life was like being able to wear a different dress every day.

I knew even then that Vanna was the real winner of the game.
Contestants were there, getting their 15 minutes and a potential to win thousands of dollars, but Vanna?
Vanna had already won.
Vanna had it all.
She was America's sweetheart.

And that's when I decided—

I was going to play *that* game instead

Something grows.

ZIIBI: *(As Pat Sajak.)* Alrighty, are you ready to spin that wheel again?

MISKOZI: I sure am, Pat!

She spins.

Projection: "Applause"
The audience cheers.

MISKOZI: "R"!

ZIIBI: *(As Pat Sajak.)* Two "R"s!

Projection: "Applause"
The audience cheers.

WAABISHKIZI turns two "R"s.

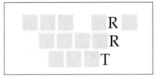

MISKOZI: And like all games on television, there was always a studio audience.
The people. The witnesses who come to revel in either the glory of someone winning the game or the glory of someone losing the game.
Who are you?
You, who laugh at the sitcom jokes.
And "ooh" at the kisses.
The ones told to "Look here and smile."
The ones heard but never seen.

You.

Behind panelled glass, watching it all unfold.
You are the ones who saw Vanna behind the
scenes.

When her makeup artist came out to powder
her face if it got shiny.

>*MISKOZI powders WAABISHKIZI's face
>and fixes her hair.*

To fix her giant hair-sprayed golden hair.
And adjust her sparkly dresses if they weren't
sitting right on her slender body.
Was she gracious?
Was she kind?
Did she expect to have her nose powdered?
Was she— /

WAABISHKIZI: *(As Vanna.)* / I need some water!
And don't forget the straw!
I can't smudge my lipstick.

MISKOZI: I didn't ever actually want the illusion to be
shattered.

Step by Step

>*Transition into Studio 2.*

>*The sound of a motorcycle revving.
>The three pose as if in a boy band.*

ALL: Step by Step!
Giiiirl

>*They dance and sing the opening to "Step
>by Step" by New Kids on the Block.*

>*ZIIBI and WAABISHKIZI begin to repeat
>a dance move over and over.*

MISKOZI stops.

MISKOZI: When you're a child, your dreams seem so much closer, don't they?

You believe that all things are possible—until someone tells you that they're not.

ZIIBI and WAABISHKIZI stop and thrust with a "UNH!"

When I was eight, I actually *believed* that I was gonna marry one of these beautiful white boys.

WAABISHKIZI: *(Whispers.)* It was Jordan.

MISKOZI: Yes. Thank you.
I mean yes, it *was* Jordan.

She sighs dreamily.

Jordan Knight.

Transition into The Living Room.

ZIIBI: *(Sings—like the beginning of a boy band song.)*
Yeeah—

ZIIBI and WAABISHKIZI begin to sing "I'll Be Loving You Forever" by New Kids on the Block, complete with side steps and snaps.

They sing underneath MISKOZI's text.

MISKOZI: I danced around my coffee table, pretending I was at their concert.
Imagining that he pulls me up on stage—because he did that. There were concerts that showed it—he did that!

So he pulls me up on stage and he gives me a rose and he sings to me and then he's so blown away by my beauty and intelligence and the age gap doesn't matter because it's the '80s and everyone's awful and no one says anything and what's 12 years when you're in love?? And then we—we keep in touch and we fall in love and we get married and /

WAABISHKIZI becomes a tabloid.

WAABISHKIZI: *(As tabloid.)* / Famed heartthrob and singer of the boy band, New Kids on the Block, Jordan Knight, caught in video porn scandal!

MISKOZI: Video ... porn? ... what?!

WAABISHKIZI: *(As tabloid.)* Sources say that Knight was caught on tape with beautiful, blonde, big-busted porn star /

MISKOZI: *(Screams.)* / NOOOO!!! WHAT!?!?!? NOOOOOOOOOO

Something grows.

MISKOZI throws herself down on a couch, grabs her Walkman and puts it on.
She sings and cries.

MISKOZI: Whyyyy, Jordan, whyyyy!?!?
(She sings through tears.)
I'll be loving you foreveeeer
Just as long as you want me to beeee

ZIIBI stops singing.
WAABISHKIZI goes to MISKOZI to comfort her.
MISKOZI is inconsolable at first—she is scream-crying.
ZIIBI plugs her ears.

ZIIBI: Geez Louise! Someone get this girl a root to
                    suck on.
                    You tryina wake up *everyone's* ancestors?!

                    WAABISHKIZI pulls off her headphones.

MISKOZI: I will never look like that.

                    WAABISHIZI pulls MISKOZI to standing.

White Boys

ZIIBI: Anyways, don't waste your tears on—

ZIIBI &
MISKOZI: White boys.

                    Transition into Studio 2.

MISKOZI: You know?
                    I always wanted their attention.
                    I did *not* want to date Native boys. The Native
                    boys were mean to me!
                    Or... you know—they were like my cousins or
                    something.
                    And that's, like... I'm not into dating my
                    cousins, you know?
                    So...
                    White boys.
                    My childhood sweetheart was a white boy.
                    With... like a white-boy name.
                    It was like Adam or Ryan or Brian or
                    something.
                    And he was *so* cute with his golden blond
                    hair and like bright blue eyes and crooked
                    smile.
                    All the girls thought he was cute.
                    We used to play the game aptly named "Boys
                    Catch Girls and Kiss."

Which is like... that's not right, you know?

Transition to The Playground.

WAABISHKIZI: *(As The White Boy.)* BOYS CATCH GIRLS AND KISSSS!!!

WAABISHKIZI becomes The White Boy and begins to chase MISKOZI around.
They giggle and flirt and play the game until WAABISHKIZI actually catches MISKOZI.
The moment is slowed and suspended as WAABISHKIZI puts her lips out to kiss MISKOZI.
The memory freezes.
MISKOZI steps out and stares at WAABISHKIZI.

MISKOZI: But of course
White boys turn into white men
And...

They move, synchronized together, telling stories of being harmed by white men.

MISKOZI: He was a...

MISKOZI &
WAABISHKIZI: Stand-in father
Touched by madness

WAABISHKIZI: Touched

MISKOZI: By his own trauma

WAABISHKIZI: Of

MISKOZI: Snakes and demon Jesuses that danced in his brain

MISKOZI &
WAABISHKIZI: We felt the back of his hand

	The front of his hand
MISKOZI:	The poisoned saliva flew onto our faces

MISKOZI &
WAABISHKIZI: The back of his hand
The front of his hand
The belts, welts, sticks and stones
Of his deep

MISKOZI: Deep

MISKOZI &
WAABISHKIZI: Seated anger
The back of his
The front of his

Gasp.

MISKOZI: The other was trusted

MISKOZI &
WAABISHKIZI: Stand-in uncle

WAABISHKIZI: He drank his poison

MISKOZI &
WAABISHKIZI: And drank his poison
And drank his

MISKOZI: His

WAABISHKIZI: His

MISKOZI &
WAABISHKIZI: Arm crept round our shoulders
Around and around

WAABISHKIZI: Coiled

MISKOZI &
WAABISHKIZI: We felt tight, burning on our skin
Pins and needles
Around and around

MISKOZI: It was only an arm

MISKOZI &
WAABISHKIZI: But
                        It felt
                        Like a whole
                        Body

> *Gasp.*
>
> *Something grows.*
>
> *The two hold their faces in the gasp and
> struggle to close their mouths.*
> *They begin a movement sequence, trying to
> heal themselves.*
> *Their mouths melt.*

Nidehem

> *ZIIBI beats the hand drum and sings as
> they move.*

ZIIBI: NI-DEH-EM   **(Nih-deh-em)**   *my heart*
                        NI-DEH-EM
                        WAY YA HEY YA HEY YO
                        NI-DEH-EM
                        NI-DEH-EM
                        WAY YA HEY YA HEY YO
                        O MY HEART
                        O MY HEART
                        SHE OPENS UP LIKE THE SEA
                        O MY HEART
                        O MY HEART
                        BREAK HER BUT YOU CAN'T BREAK ME
                        NI-DEH-EM
                        NI-DEH-EM
                        WAY YA HEY YA HEY YO
                        NI-DEH-EM

NI-DEH-EM
WAY YA HEY YA HEY YO
WAY YA HEY YA HEY YO
WAY YA HEY YA HEY

Transition into The Living Room.

WAABISHKIZI: You wanna watch TV?

MISKOZI nods as they settle into their TV-watching position.
ZIIBI becomes the news.

ZIIBI: *(As the news.)* Good evening.

It was a bloody day at the Mohawk Indian community in Oka, Quebec near Montreal.
Provincial police in riot gear stormed the barricades the Mohawks had set up.
There were clouds of tear gas.
A hail of bullets.
And in the midst of the battle, a policeman was killed.
All this because of a dispute over a piece of forest the Indians claim is theirs.

MISKOZI and WAABISHKIZI are not paying attention.
MISKOZI is playing with or looking at or is fascinated by WAABISHKIZI'S hair.

MISKOZI: I wish I was a blonde.

Wheel of Fortune theme song, in vocables.

Transition into Studio 1.

Projection: "Applause"
The audience cheers.

WAABISHKIZI becomes Vanna.
ZIIBI becomes Pat.

MISKOZI is excited to have another crack at the game.

ZIIBI: (*As Pat Sajak.*) Welcome back.
As you can see, we have three letters on the board.
And uh Truth. Truth is the category.
And Mis–Mis–Missy, it's your turn to start.

MISKOZI: It's Miskozi.

ZIIBI: (*As Pat Sajak.*) And that is great.

MISKOZI: I'll spin.

> *She spins.*
> *Projection: "Applause"*
> *The audience cheers.*

ZIIBI: (*As Pat Sajak.*) Oh! It looks as though we have a privilege prize if you get this letter.
This is the "Have More Fun" package—which we all know you do *get* as a blonde. Isn't that right, Vanna?

> *Projection: "Laugh"*
> *The audience laughs.*

> *WAABISHKIZI as VANNA stays smiling wide.*

WAABISHKIZI: (*As Vanna.*) That's right, Pat.

MISKOZI: (*As Pat Sajak.*) Say, Vanna, why don't you tell our contestant all about the fun benefits you get?

WAABISHKIZI: (*As Vanna.*) Well, Pat, I would definitely say that I get way more male attention, I can dye my hair with Kool-Aid and there's always someone who looks like me in my favourite movies. So that's fun.

ZIIBI: *(As Pat Sajak.)* Wow. Just wow. Sounds like a
                   great prize.
                   Okay, Michelin. What'll it be?

                   MISKOZI regards the board.

MISKOZI: "H"?

ZIIBI: *(As Pat Sajak.)* Oooh, I'm sorry, no "H."

                   Projection: "Boo"
                   The audience boos.

                   *WAABISHKIZI as VANNA makes a "darn
                   it" motion with her arm.*

ZIIBI: *(As Pat Sajak.)* Looks like it's an at-home hair
                   bleach kit from Zellers for you.
                   We'll be right back after these messages.

Dream—Fingertips

                   The In-Between Place.

                   Smoke.
                   Embers.
                   Sparks.

                   Searching.

                   *MISKOZI begins to slowly repeat the lost
                   movement.*

MISKOZI: My feet are cold.

WAABISHKIZI: Tell me.

MISKOZI: I don't know where to start looking.

WAABISHKIZI: What are you looking for?

MISKOZI: I'm not sure, but I feel like I just had it.

WAABISHKIZI: We need answers.

MISKOZI: I just had it, I know I did.
                It was just here.
                I just had it.

        The movement builds faster,
        It begins to rain.
        The river swells and submerges them.
        They both become fish.

        There is stillness; a suspended moment
        underwater.
        The river is where the truth is.
        ZIIBI flows in as the Trout fish.

ZIIBI: (*As the Trout.*) Dreamworld is the mirror for
                prophecy and truth.
                Your debwewin,
                sister. **(deh-bway-win)**   *Truth*

                Nishke!   **(Nishgay)**   *Look!*
                Gshkozi   **(Shkozih)**   *Open your eyes*

MISKOZI: And there is a great big heaviness
                Hanging
                Swinging in the air above me

MISKOZI &
WAABISHKIZI: Hanging

MISKOZI: I snatch at it with invisible hands
                Hands that are dirty
                Hands that are

MISKOZI &
WAABISHKIZI: Clean

MISKOZI: Hands that reach
                Reach for missing pieces in the air
                Missing voices
                Reaching for words
                And whispers

                      And

MISKOZI &
WAABISHKIZI: Fingertips

MISKOZI: That draw circles around my eyes, my heart
              Nshkiizhigoo **(Nish-gee-zhih-go)** *My eyes*
              Ni-deh-em   **(Neh-deh-em)**   *My heart*

ALL: Fingertips

MISKOZI: That take years to trace the curves of my body
              and soul
              I am searching for my skin

WAABISHKIZI: But what will it cost us?

              The rain falls harder.
              The two are reaching,
              Reaching
              For the surface.

              ZIIBI exhales.
              The river suddenly retreats as the rain
              turns into audience cheering and the wheel
              spinning.

              Transition into Studio 1.

              WAABISHKI has become Vanna White
              again and is standing in front of the board.
              ZIIBI has become Pat Sajak.

ZIIBI: *(As Pat Sajak.)* Welcome back. Still only three
              letters on the board and uh... Misherbert, it's
              your turn to spin.

MISKOZI: Wha—?
              That's not even a name.

ZIIBI: *(As Pat Sajak.)* Sure isn't.

MISKOZI: What just happened?

ZIIBI: *(As Pat Sajak.)* It's your turn to spin.

MISKOZI: Oh...
              Oh okay.
              Yeah! I'll spin.

              She spins.

              Projection: "Applause"
              The audience cheers.

MISKOZI: Um ooh... "N"?

ZIIBI: *(As Pat Sajak.)* One "N"!

MISKOZI: Yes!

              Projection: "Applause"
              The audience cheers.

              WAABISHKIZI turns the letter.

ZIIBI: *(As Pat Sajak.)* Would you like to spin or solve?

MISKOZI: Definitely spin!

              She spins.

              Projection: "Applause"
              The audience cheers.

MISKOZI: "D"!

ZIIBI: *(As Pat Sajak.)* Ooh I'm sorry. No "D"s.

              Projection: "Boo"
              The audience boos.

> *WAABISHKIZI makes a "darn it" motion with her arm.*

MISKOZI: Really? With the booing?

ZIIBI: *(As Pat Sajak.)* We'll be right back after these messages.

MISKOZI: But we just had a commercial break.

> *As ZIIBI is flowing off in another direction:*

ZIIBI: *(As Pat Sajak.)* Gotta sell those ThighMasters somehow!

MISKOZI: Wait!
                Wait—I just need another chance...
                Please?!
                Pat!?
                Pat!!

> *WAABISHKIZI, seeing that MISKOZI is clearly upset, leaves the board and comes to her.*

> *She holds her.*

WAABISHKIZI: Shhhhh.
                We'll have another chance.

> *Transition into The Living Room.*

> *WAABISHKIZI takes MISKOZI to the couch.*

Gramma's Hands

> *MISKOZI and WAABISHKIZI stretch in sync and lie on the couch and fall asleep.*

> *Beat.*

ZIIBI bangs the drum hard.
Loud.
MISKOZI and WAABISHKIZI wake up
and groan.
They slide off the couch.

MISKOZI &
WAABISHKIZI: Grammmaaaaa!

ZIIBI: *(As Gramma.)* What

MISKOZI: So loud.

ZIIBI: *(As Gramma.)* What? No. It's fine. You know I'm goin' deaf.
Time to get up anyways.
Grampa'll make you Cheez Whiz toast and tea.

MISKOZI &
WAABISHKIZI: But it's Saturdaaaaay.

ZIIBI: *(As Gramma.)* Shush. Time to get up.

The two girls stand and they all begin a baking sequence, their hands dipped into bowls of flour. (There does not actually have to be flour.)

MISKOZI: Gramma was always baking
And cooking.
She would cook up the moose meat that Grandpa would hunt.
One time I brought some to school and /

WAABISHKIZI: *(As Vegetarian Girl.)* / Eew. You're gonna eat that? Killing animals is wrong. You wouldn't eat a dog, would you?

MISKOZI: ...I didn't really like it, though.

But her baking was *so* good.
She was always baking.

Flour everywhere!
White grains like sand sifted through the air.
Heavy like rain fell into our hands.

MISKOZI &
WAABISHKIZI: Flour was everywhere.

MISKOZI: In our hair.
On our cheeks.
Up to our elbows in it.

> *WAABISHKIZI looks at her arms.*
> *MISKOZI does the same.*

MISKOZI: At school I would sometimes get made fun of
for being brown.
I didn't actually realize that I was brown until
some shitty little kid told me.
And sometimes they would say things like—

WAABISHKIZI: *(To herself.)* Why are you so dark?

> *They continue to look at their arms.*
> *MISKOZI begins to cover her arms in more*
> *flour.*

MISKOZI: I wish I wasn't brown.

> *ZIIBI/Gramma snaps her head towards*
> *MISKOZI and whacks her with a mixing*
> *spoon.*

WAABISHKIZI: OW!!

ZIIBI: *(As Gramma.)* I don't ever want to hear you
say that again!
You hear me, Miskozi?

MISKOZI: Yeah Gramma, geez.

ZIIBI: *(As Gramma.)* You be proud of your skin, my
girl. Be proud.

> *MISKOZI & WAABISHKIZI nod.*

They return to the flour.
MISKOZI begins to wipe off her arms as best she can.
WAABISHKIZI does the same.
ZIIBI stays in the flour as Gramma but does similar movements to the two.

MISKOZI: Gramma was an artist
Together we would make masterpieces together
Cookies, bannock, pies, biscuits...
She showed me how to dance with the dough

Knead
Knead
Pat
Roll
Cut
Cut
Cut

Her wrinkled hands were quick
Her berry-picking hands
Her Bingo-dabbing hands
Her beading hands
Her smoking hands
Her slapping hands

Her hands were quick always

MISKOZI &
WAABISHKIZI: Knead
Knead
Pat
Roll
Cut
Cut
Cut

WAABISHKIZI: *(Underneath MISKOZI's text below.)* Knead
Knead
Pat

                    Roll
                    Cut
                    Cut
                    Cut

MISKOZI: It was like a ritual we'd do together.
                    Deep in the mess of dough.
                    Scraps from her masterpiece would go onto
                    my table so that I could practise.

MISKOZI &
WAABISHKIZI: Knead
                    Knead
                    Pat
                    Roll
                    Cut
                    Cut
                    Cut

MISKOZI &
WAABISHKIZI: Knead
                    Knead
                    Pat
                    Roll
                    Cut
                    Cut
                    Cut

                    Knead
                    Knead
                    Pat
                    Roll
                    Cut
                    Cut
                    Cut!

                            They are not baking anymore.
                            It escalates.
                            They turn to ZIIBI/Gramma.

ALL: Why are you crying?!

ZIIBI/Gramma spills the flour.
They all stare at each other.

Breath.

They all repeat the lost movement.

ALL: Shhh
                        Put it away now
                        Put it away
                        Hide it
                        Hide it like treasure
                        Stuff it in places you'll never look to find
                        Inside your body
                        Inside your mind
                        Sink it deep into the divine darkness
                        Where no one
                        Will think
                        To look
                        Shhh

Something grows.

MISKOZI &
WAABISHKIZI: It's all right.

ZIIBI/Gramma sweeps up the flour.
The two circle around and watch her.

MISKOZI: Gramma was silent like I was silent.

WAABISHKIZI: *(Whispering.)* White boys turn into white men.

MISKOZI: Her pain was like my pain.

WAABISHKIZI: *(Whispering.)* White boys turn into white men.

MISKOZI: And somehow we found all the ways to block out each other's pain.

WAABISHKIZI: *(Whispering.)* White boys turn into white men.

MISKOZI: With our own.

> *ZIIBI places her hand in the flour and makes a white handprint across her mouth.*

MISKOZI: I know your face.

> *Breath.*

White Girls

> *Transition into Studio 2.*

There's Nothing More Dangerous

> *ZIIBI walks past WAABISHKIZI and MISKOZI and sings.*

ZIIBI: THERE'S NOTHING MORE DANGEROUS
                THAN A WHITE WOMAN

> *WAABISHKIZI and MISKOZI get knocked back to childhood.*

THERE'S NOTHING MORE DANGEROUS
THAN A WHITE WOMAN
PUT YOUR FISTS IN THE AIR
TAKE YOUR MARCHES OUT THERE
PUT YOUR PUSSY HATS ON
SING YOUR WHITE WOMAN SONGS
STAND BY YOUR MEN WHILE THEY
ABUSE THEIR POWER
WEAPONIZING TEARS AND THREATS
ON THE HOUR
THERE'S NOTHING MORE DANGEROUS
THAN A WHITE WOMAN
SAY THEIR NAME

THAT BLACK WOMAN LOST HER CHILD
FOR YOU
THE RIOTS ARE STARTING UP
AND IT'S JUST TOO MUCH FOR YOU
THE FRONT LINES ARE SCARY
BROWN VOICES DON'T CARRY
YOU'RE A KEYBOARD WARRIOR WITH
FILTERS THAT VARY
IT LOOKS LIKE ANGER BUT FEELS LIKE
SLIGHT
WHEN NOT ALL WOMEN ARE ALLOWED
IN YOUR FIGHT
WHERE WERE YOU WHEN OUR SISTER
TINA WAS FAILED
OR WHEN STANDING ROCK NEEDED
SOME FIGHT TO PREVAIL
BLACK LIVES MATTER AT THE PRIDE
PARADE
DID YOU PUT YOUR FISTS UP OR TELL
THEM TO MOVE THAT TRUCK
THERE'S NOTHING MORE DANGEROUS
THAN A WHITE WOMAN
THERE'S NOTHING MORE DANGEROUS
THAN A WHITE WOMAN
THERE'S NOTHING MORE DANGEROUS

ZIIBI flows off.

Transition into The Playground.

MIKSOZI and WAABISHKIZI begin enacting the scene from 1989 Disney's The Little Mermaid, *where Ariel and Flounder are exploring.*

MISKOZI and WAABISHKIZI (as Little White Girl) sing the lines from "Daughters of Triton" that introduce Ariel. Then:

WAABISHKIZI: *(As Little White Girl.)* Ariel!!
(She then plays Flounder.) Ariel, wait for me . . .

MISKOZI plays Ariel.

MISKOZI: Hurry up, Flounder!

WAABISHKIZI: *(As Little White Girl.)* Wait for me.

MISKOZI: Look, it's over there! Isn't it wonderful?

WAABISHKIZI: *(As Little White Girl.)* Yeah… sure… it–it's awesome. Can we go now?

MISKOZI: You're not afraid, are you?

WAABISHKIZI: *(As Little White Girl.)* Who, me? No way. It's just, it, err… it looks—wet in there.
Yeah. And I think I might be getting a cold. Listen. *(Coughs unconvincingly.)*

MISKOZI: Oh, Fl… *(She stops and looks at her.)*
I think you needa be more scared.
Like MORE you know?

            WAABISHKIZI as Little White Girl sighs in frustration and sits down.

MISKOZI: What's wrong?

WAABISHKIZI: *(As Little White Girl.)* I just don't understand why I have to be Flounder.

MISKOZI: Well, because we need a Flounder.

WAABISHKIZI: *(As Little White Girl.)* Why can't YOU be Flounder?

MISKOZI: Um … because it was *my* idea.

WAABISHKIZI: *(As Little White Girl.)* I just think… *(She twirls her light hair around her finger.)*

MISKOZI: What?

WAABISHKIZI: *(As Little White Girl.)* I mean, I don't think you can be Ariel.

MISKOZI: Why not?!

WAABISHKIZI: *(As Little White Girl.)* Well, cuz you... cuz you're...

MISKOZI: What?

WAABISHKIZI: *(As Little White Girl.)* You have brown hair and Ariel has red hair, so—

MISKOZI: So? We don't know anyone with red hair. Your hair's not red either.
Plus I'm the better singer, so—

WAABISHKIZI: *(As Little White Girl.)* So—

MISKOZI: So—

MISKOZI &
WAABISHKIZI: Soooooooo
UGH!

WAABISHKIZI: *(As Little White Girl.)* You're so bossy!

MISKOZI: I don't want you in my play anyways!

> *They walk off in opposite directions.*

> *We hear them both singing Ariel's vocal part, the ending of it sounds angry and competitive—who can be louder?*

> *Transition into Studio 2.*

> *They come back out.*
> *WAABISHKIZI is shaking sleigh bells.*

MISKOZI: A solo?
Me?
Well—okay!

> *She steps forward to take centre stage to sing the opening to "Rudolph the Red Nosed Reindeer."*

WAABISHKIZI as Tiffany Smith comes out and takes over, enthusiastically singing the opening of the song.

MISKOZI, defeated, circles her.

WAABISHKIZI/Tiffany Smith continues to dance around and be beautiful, singing "Rudolph the Red-Nosed Reindeer."

MISKOZI: Tiffany Smith.
That was her name.
Tiffany.
Smith.
White girl who came in and stole my solo.
She was so pretty.
And tall.

This kept happening!
I kept getting replaced or looked over for white girls.

Like—okay...

(To WAABISHKIZI who is still singing—)

OKAY!

WAABISHKIZI stops singing and ditches the bells.

MISKOZI: *Wizard of Oz* auditions.
Fifth grade.
The teacher asked who wanted to audition for Dorothy.

Both MISKOZI and WAABISHKIZI's hands shoot straight up.
They go to their audition positions.

And do an identical routine to a section of "Come Out, Come Out" from Metro-Goldwyn-Mayer's The Wizard of Oz.

> *MISKOZI and WAABISHKIZI sing the verse of "Munchkinland" that contains the tricky "switch/pitch/unhitch/witch/itch/hitch" rhymes.*

> *They both continue to do the routine, physically, picking up pace.*

MISKOZI: I was so proud.
And I practised so much.
Over and over again, until I could do the whole thing without messing up.
And in that audition—
At that moment—
I was Judy Garland!
The next day they were pulling us up one by one to give us our parts.
They came up to me
And they were so excited
To offer me the role... of the Tin Man.

> *MISKOZI stops, but WAABISHKIZI continues with the routine as it expands, and she becomes the white girl who got the part and does a movement sequence through* The Wizard of Oz.

I was devastated, so I... turned it down, thinking maybe I could hold out for the Witch. But then they offered me the Scarecrow and, like... I just couldn't look cute in straw, you know? It's itchy! I have allergies!
I just... I did so well, and it was clear they wanted me to play a lead. Just... not Dorothy. I guess they didn't want a brown-skinned Dorothy. All the white parents probably would have freaked out.
So... they covered me in a Cowardly Lion costume instead.

> *Beat.*

Then MISKOZI begins to sing the last line of the song "Somewhere Over the Rainbow." She is interrupted by WAABISHKIZI as White Girl Dorothy, who finishes the line, loudly.

The two skip side-by-side down the yellow brick road.
MISKOZI is miserable.

Projection: "Applause"
The audience cheers.
They bow.

Choose Something

Transition into The Living Room.

The two sit huddled in the middle.
They stare out at the TV.

MISKOZI: So whaddya want to watch?

WAABISHKIZI shrugs.

MISKOZI: Well, we have to choose something.

WAABISHKIZI shrugs again.

MISKOZI: Well, you're helpful.

WAABISHKIZI mocks her.
They nudge each other in annoyance.

MISKOZI: I miss Gramma and Grandpa.

WAABISHKIZI nods.

ZIIBI: White fur. Brown-skinned. Flowered dress.

MISKOZI: What if we went to the park?

WAABISKIZI gives an exaggerated exasperated sigh and dramatically falls back.

ZIIBI becomes the news.

ZIIBI: (*As The News.*) During the crisis at Camp Ipperwash, former Ontario Premier Mike Harris was heard to say:
"I want the fucking Indians out of the park," hours before police moved in and shot unarmed protester Dudley George dead.

MISKOZI stands up.

MISKOZI: Why would /

WAABISHKI: / What if we played a game?

MISKOZI: What?

WAABISHKI: We should buy a vowel!

MISKOZI: Um, okay.
But did you just hear /

Wheel of Fortune theme song, in vocables.

Transition into Studio 1.

Projection: "Applause"
The audience cheers.

WAABISHKI has become Vanna White again and is standing in front of the board. ZIIBI has become Pat Sajak.

MISKOZI: Um—okay.
I'd like to buy an "O."

ZIIBI: (*As Pat Sajak.*) Two "O"s! Look at you!

Projection: "Applause"
The audience cheers.

WAABISHKIZI/Vanna turns the letters.

ZIIBI: *(As Pat Sajak.)* You are *really* making Vanna work here and the stakes have never been higher!

MISKOZI feels the pressure.

ZIIBI: *(As Pat Sajak.)* So ... are you ready to solve?

She considers the puzzle.

MISKOZI: ...no.
                I don't know what this is trying to say...

                WAABISHKIZI, embarrassed, slides over to MISKOZI, dropping her Vanna.

WAABISHKIZI: You wanted to play a game

MISKOZI: I know but... I don't think this is helping me find what I'm looking for.

WAABISHKIZI: Are you sure?

MISKOZI: ...no

WAABISHKIZI: Well, I think we have to keep playing if we want to win.
                And we're *so* close.
                What if...
                What if we spun the wheel?
                Then we can guess again.

                MISKOZI nods.
                WAABISHKIZI smiles and claps her hands together and takes her place at the board as Vanna.

MISKOZI: I'd like to spin.

                    She spins again.

                    Projection: "Applause"
                    The audience cheers.

ZIIBI: *(As Pat Sajak.)* Oh look! Another privilege prize. This one is "Etiquette."
Yes, etiquette—so you can code-switch as you please and impress all of the nice white parents.

WAABISHKIZI: *(As Vanna.)* Everyone loves good grammar!

ZIIBI: *(As Pat Sajak.)* They sure do, Vanna. They sure do.
And let me tell ya, it's also extremely helpful when talking to the police. That rez accent that would have gotten you roughed up and / or *(Out the side of their mouth.)* killed, will completely disappear!
All right, what'll it be, sweetheart?

                    MISKOZI walks closer to the puzzle.

MISKOZI: "S."

ZIIBI: *(As Pat Sajak.)* One "S"!

                    Projection: "Applause"
                    The audience cheers.

                    WAABISHKIZI turns the letter.

ZIIBI: *(As Pat Sajak.)* Pick up that prize. You will be the most skillful and articulate and possibly alive Indian at the dinner table and in class, assuming you go to college, which you probably won't.
Okee dokey, what next?

MISKOZI: I–I'll spin.

                    MISKOZI spins.

MISKOZI: "M"?

ZIIBI: *(As Pat Sajak.)* Oooh, sorry there's no "M."

                    Projection: "Boo"
                    The audience boos.

                    WAABISHKIZI walks up and puts her arm around MISKOZI.

WAABISHKIZI: Let's play something else.

                    The game disappears.

Pocahontas and Ariel Swim into a Bar

                    Transition into Studio 2.

                    MISKOZI and WAABISHKIZI sit.
                    MISKOZI recites the opening of "Just Around the Riverbend" from Disney's 1995 Pocahontas *as a monologue, then she softly sings the last two lines of the first verse.*

                    MISKOZI takes a beat. She and WAABISHKIZI look at each other and then burst into the chorus.

                    They sing the entire first chorus of the song.

Loudly. Fully embodying the song.

MISKOZI: Okay, okay, so honestly, when Pocahontas came out, I knew that I should have seen myself in her, but I didn't. I didn't look like her. She didn't look... like me. Like if being Native meant talking to trees, jumping off cliffs and not kissing your best friend even though she was clearly the hottest person in your tribe—

ZIIBI: *(As a cough.)* Kocoum.

MISKOZI: What?

WAABISHKIZI: What?

MISKOZI: Did you say something?

WAABISHKIZI: Did *you* say something?

MISKOZI: Oh, we're not doing this again.

ZIIBI: *(As a louder cough.)* Kocoum.

> *The two look around, confused, then back at each other.*
> *Shrug and mumble/ad-lib "I don't know," "It was the cat or something," "Theatre ghost?" etc.*

ZIIBI: Ugh!

MISKOZI: Anyways, I also wasn't like an Indian princess, "protecting her people..." I mean my great-grandfather *was* chief...

> *WAABISHKIZI gasps excitedly.*

...but that doesn't mean... wait—does it mean?... Maybe I am an Indian princess! Maybe I've been an Indian princess this whole time!

WAABISHKIZI: *(Ready to take the role of Pocahontas.)* YOU THINK YOU OWN—/

ZIIBI: *(As Pocahontas.)* / Ahhh hey hey I'm here! I got this one, thanks.

MISKOZI: Pocahontas?!

ZIIBI: *(As Pocahontas.)* ...yes.

She stands stoically.

MISKOZI: Oh, wow! Okay! Um, can I ask you... are you a *real* Indian princess? Like... are you a princess because your father was chief? Or is it because ... Disney made you one?

ZIIBI: *(As Pocahontas.)* Well... let's just start with the fact that Pocahontas is *not* my real name and I was more like ehh, 10 or 11 when this story, uh, "happened." I was actually kidnapped.

Yeah. Oh, and baptized and given a new name and married off to a white tobacco farmer who exploited me for my tobacco harvesting knowledge and then I, uh—I actually died tragically, quite young.

MISKOZI: What!?

ZIIBI: *(As Pocahontas.)* I should have married Kocoum.

Also, we don't have princesses or anything like that. Our leadership systems were far more advanced than what you have now.

Beat.

MISKOZI: ... Ssso you're saying I can't be an Indian princess?

WAABISHKIZI (as Ariel) swims forward.

WAABISHKIZI: *(As Ariel.)* You can if you marry a handsome prince who you save from drowning.

MISKOZI: Ariel!?

WAABISHKIZI: *(As Ariel.)* There might be some... sacrifices though.
But I promise it'll be worth it.

MISKOZI: What sacrifices?

WAABISHKIZI: *(As Ariel.)* What does it matter when you're the most beautiful and powerful Indi-yaa...

> *ZIIBI/Pocahontas shakes her head, WAABISHKIZI/Ariel tries to pivot.*

WAABISHKIZI: *(As Ariel.)* ... aaaborigiNaaatiiiFirstNashhIndigenous princess around?

MISKOZI: I mean, she's got a point. It would just be easier to marry a prince and become a princess.

WAABISHKIZI: *(As Ariel.)* Exactly!

MISKOZI: And like—it's totally possible. William's my age.

WAABISHKIZI: *(As Ariel.)* Sure!

MISKOZI: And I'm sure the royals aren't *that* racist, right?

> *No one says a word.*

MISKOZI: Right??

> *After a moment, ZIIBI (as Pocahontas) takes MISKOZI by the shoulders.*

ZIIBI: *(As Pocahontas.)* Oh. You're going to need to read a lot of books.

MISKOZI: Wha—?

WAABISHKIZI/Ariel swims in between them.

WAABISHKIZI: *(As Ariel.)* It's fine. Come with me.
You can trust me!
I have a tail. See.
See my tail.
See.

ZIIBI: *(As Pocahontas.)* We see your tail, fish! Lucky I don't smoke you and eat you for dinner.
(To MISKOZI.) Come. I can show you your truth.

WAABISHKIZI: *(As Ariel.)* Ffffish?!
How dare you!
I am a Queen!

ZIIBI: *(As Pocahontas.)* Of where? Of what? Of who?

WAABISHKIZI: *(As Ariel.)* I... I don't need to answer to *you*!
(To MISKOZI.) Look at me. Listen.

She sings the vocal part from The Little Mermaid *and gets MISKOZI to join her. She lets MISKOZI take over.*

See! See how beautiful you sound as a princess!

MISKOZI reaches the end note and she stands in her glory.
ZIIBI/Pocahontas shakes her head.

ZIIBI: *(As Pocahontas.)* Okay. I'm gonna go find a lake to jump into or a cliff to be... stoic on, I don't know. Call me when you ditch the fish.

She leaves.

MISKOZI and WAABISHKIZI embrace each other, giggling.

Dream—Submersion

Transition into the In-Between Place.

The river rushes.
MISKOZI and WAABISHKIZI are submerged.
ZIIBI flows on as the Trout fish.

ZIIBI: *(As the Trout.)* Gda Boonzi naabi epiichi giizhaa eyaawat-yin
(Gda bohn-zih naah-bih eh-pee-chay gee-zhaa eh-ya-wot-yin)
Stop searching for what you already have

Nishke!
Nishke!   **(Nishkay)**   *Look!*
Gshkozi   **(Shkozih)**   *Open your eyes*
Gi-bgizoomgad epiichi biinjii'yii debwewin-nim
(Gih-bgiz-ohm-gad eh-pee-chih been-jee-yuh-ee deh-bway-win-im)
You swim while inside your truth

WAABISHKIZI begins to vocalize "There's a Place" (the opening song.)
MISKOZI joins her.
Then ZIIBI.
The sound fills all of the spaces.

The dream begins to shift.

The two sit side by side and fall asleep on each other.
The song transforms into the sound of a Greyhound.

Move

Transition to a Greyhound in Studio 2

A bump wakes them up.
The two do a movement sequence as if in a tight space, but routinely come back to sitting.

MISKOZI:

When I was 15, I had to take the Greyhound by myself at night from a city I didn't know.
I was a little scared
Tried to be brave.
It felt like
Nobody wanted me to sit next to them
Which, I guess is normal
People don't like strangers getting too close.
There was a blonde woman, sleeping,
Slumped over sideways, taking up both seats.
I stopped because I hoped that she would maybe wake up and you know, move over.
My anxiety had me frozen.
I looked up and there was this big Native guy standing in front of me.
"You wanna sit down?" he asked.
I nodded.
He then very swiftly jammed his hand under the side of her head and threw her over towards the window and said:

MISKOZI &
WAABISHKIZI: "Move!"

MISKOZI:

I jumped.
The woman just moaned a little and, like... kept sleeping?

WAABISHKIZI: Thank you

MISKOZI: "You're welcome"

And he went back to his seat.

I still don't know how to feel about that interaction.
I come from violence, so the

MISKOZI &
WAABISHKIZI: Violence

MISKOZI: of it made me uncomfortable.
I mean, he put his hands on a woman without consent and literally tossed her over.
That wasn't okay.
But in another way, I saw a big Indian protecting his little Indian sister. Giving her space. Making space for her.
I don't have brothers.

I didn't really grow up with solid masculine figures, so...
It felt like an act of kindness.

For me.
Not for her.
When she woke up, she was none the wiser and offered me a donut from her cooler, so...
I mean, I guess she was fine?

> MISKOZI looks towards WAABISHKIZI as if she was the woman.
> WAABISHKIZI gives a sleepy thumbs-up.

See?

I didn't tell anyone when I got home.
I just sort of kept it to myself.

Sometimes I think about him
And wonder if he's okay.

> The two get off the bus and watch it pull away.

Alabaster Baby

> *The heart.*
>
> *Heartbeat.*
>
> *WAABISHKIZI is turning and posing as if on display.*

MISKOZI: White women.
White.
Women.
Their alabaster skin.
Cream.
Pale.
Ivory.
There are, like, a million words for "white."
Pearl.
Iridescent.
They all sound soft.
Like lace.
Not like brown.
Brown is like...
Brown is like leather
Brown was always dirty.
Soiled.
Ruined.
Ugly.
The crayon no one wanted.
(Beat.)
Shit.
I was shit.

> *Something grows.*
>
> *Transition into The Playground.*

MISKOZI: But something about being next to a white woman made me feel—somehow accepted.

> *ZIIBI begins to sing "Leather and Lace" by Stevie Nicks.*

The two stand far apart from each other but move together with intricacy — taking a long time to come together during this exchange.
They dance/move together.

MISKOZI: My first relationship was with a white woman. We were teenagers.

WAABISHKIZI: Went to different schools.

MISKOZI: But lived in the same neighbourhood in the city.
            And I used to use all of those beautiful, soft words to describe her.

WAABISHKIZI: She was tall.
            With long, blonde hair—

MISKOZI: I imagined us braiding it together.

MISKOZI &
WAABISHKIZI: Our long, long hair.

MISKOZI: She smiled at me.

WAABISHKIZI: A sweet, strawberry-pink-tinted, blushing, Lip Smackers smile.

They both smack their lips.

MISKOZI: I discovered myself in her
            We were a playground together
            Climbing up and around
            Sliding down
            Swinging
            We played so many games to get to where we wanted to be
            Never speaking out loud
            Our sin
            I turned inside-out
            And became whatever she wanted me to be
            I was drowning in her

MISKOZI drowns in WAABISHKIZI.
They explore each other underwater.

Eventually, they both come up, gasping
for air.
WAABISHKIZI clings to MISKOZI—
MISKOZI delicately tries to maneuver
around her.
They switch.
·The more this goes on, the clingier the
other becomes and the harder it becomes to
remove the other.

MISKOZI: There was no end
                  I saw none
                  I only saw her
                  She only saw me

WAABISHKIZI: *(As The Girlfriend.)* It's only you

MISKOZI: Living co-dependently
                  Following each other's lead
                  Hand to hand
                  Palm to finger
                  Skin to lips
                  I only saw her
                  She only saw me

WAABISHKIZI: *(As The Girlfriend.)* It's only you

MISKOZI: The addiction grew
                  Unhealthy silences and blame
                  Rolling away
                  Sliding away
                  Climbing apart
                  Clinging and clawing at each other
                  Manipulation and mind games
                  Emotional strings
                  I only saw her
                  She only saw me

WAABISHKIZI: *(As The Girlfriend.)* No! I don't like girls.
It's only *you.*

MISKOZI: Until she didn't.
Until I found out she was fucking some white
guy behind my back.

WAABISHKIZI leaves.

Something grows.

MISKOZI: But it was too late.
I was already in her world.
Made a home there.
A nest there.
I had nowhere else to go.
I left everyone else behind.

She turns to where her girlfriend left.
She loses her breath.

I left everyone else behind.
For you.

She collapses.
Echoes of "Leather and Lace" can be heard.

Pills & Pins & Alcohol & Ice Cream

Transition into The Living Room.

MISKOZI is still on the floor.
*WAABISHKIZI enters and tries to get her
up.*
*She is more forceful this time and finally
gets her sitting up.*
*They stare at each other before beginning a
hand-clapping game.*

*As they play, each time it increases in
intensity.*

MISKOZI &
WAABISHKIZI: PILLS AND PINS AND ALCOHOL AND
ICE CREAM
TALK IS CHEAP AND SO IS MY SOUL
GOING OUT LIKE A HURRICANE
BLOOD IS ON MY HANDS
AROUND AND AROUND AND AROUND
WE GO AND

PILLS AND PINS AND ALCOHOL AND
ICE CREAM
TALK IS CHEAP AND SO IS MY SOUL
GOING OUT LIKE A HURRICANE
BLOOD IS ON MY HANDS
AROUND AND AROUND AND AROUND
WE GO AND

PILLS AND PINS AND ALCOHOL AND
ICE CREAM
TALK IS CHEAP AND SO IS MY SOUL
GOING OUT LIKE A HURRICANE
BLOOD IS ON MY HANDS
AROUND AND AROUND AND AROUND
AND AROUND
AND AROUND AND AROUND AND

They scream.
It goes dark.

In the darkness.

WAABISHKIZI: I need

MISKOZI: Comfort

WAABISHKIZI: I need

MISKOZI: Warmth

WAABISHKIZI: I need

MISKOZI: My home

The Numbing

> *Transition into Studio 2.*
>
> *MISKOZI and WAABISHKIZI lie in the middle, their bodies twisted around each other.*

MISKOZI: Numb me

> *ZIIBI beats the drum.*
> *The two bodies respond to the beats.*
>
> *Almost animalistic.*
>
> *ZIIBI sings.*

ZIIBI: WATCH MY WORLD MOVE TO YOUR BEAT
SEE MY HEART FALL AT YOUR FEET
FEEL MY SKIN CHARGE WHEN WE TOUCH
AS WE OPEN, EXPOSE AND RUSH

GIVE ME SOMETHING
I'VE LOST CONTROL
A REMINDER OF WHAT WE KNOW

> *MISKOZI and WAABISHKIZI speak over the drumbeat*

MISKOZI: Her skin
Was warm
And soft
Light
Airy
Whipped cream kisses
She would open her mouth
And rose petals came pouring out
And we bathed in them
Together

WAABISHKIZI: We remained in them
                Together

MISKOZI: She wasn't lace
                She was orchid
                Lilies
                Labia flowers

MISKOZI &
WAABISHKIZI: Drenched in honey

ZIIBI: WATCH MY WORLD MOVE TO YOUR
                BEAT
                SEE MY HEART FALL AT YOUR FEET
                FEEL MY SKIN CHANGE AS I BLUSH
                A SUDDEN MOVEMENT
                A SUDDEN CRUSSSSH

MISKOZI: His eyes were ocean blue
                Lagoon blue
                Musings from his lips
                Would hit my body
                And heal the places that had scars
                He tasted like what I thought love looked like

MISKOZI &
WAABISHKIZI: And I
                Drank
                Every
                Drop

                    WAABISHKIZI sings comes in and out
                    during the following:

ZIIBI: WATCH MY WORLD MOVE TO YOUR
                BEAT
                SEE MY HEART FALL AT YOUR FEET

                FEEL MY SKIN CHARGE WHEN WE
                TOUCH
                TAKE YOUR MOVEMENT, I TAKE YOUR
                RUSH

ALL: GIVE ME SOMETHING, I'VE LOST CON-
        TROL

ZIIBI: A REMINDER OF WHAT WE KNOW

MISKOZI: She was holographic /
            And round
            Used me to wipe up her tears

WAABISHKIZI: / She was rainbow hair
                Gap-toothed
                Made me laugh

MISKOZI: They were glitter /
            And bowties
            We cried together

WAABISHKIZI: / He was muscles
                And tattoos
                And lied about having a kid

MISKOZI: They were sweet / but guarded
            So we fell into crimson & clover
            Over and over and over

WAABISHKIZI: / He was strong
                And hated that I didn't want a threesome
                And tried to convince me
                Over and over and over

MISKOZI &
WAABISHKIZI: Over and over and over!

ZIIBI: WATCH ME WORLD ...MOVE
        WATCH MY HEART ...FALL

ALL: FALL

My Moccasins

>
> *Transition into the In-Between Place.*
>
> *MISKOZI and WAABISHKIZI sit, their legs doing fancy dance moves.*
>
> *ZIIBI vocalizes "There's a Place."*

MISKOZI: We took each other for granted.
I never understood them fully.
I feel like we stared at each other for a long time.
They were beautiful.
Soft in all the right places.
Rough in all the right places.
Delicate dips of colour dancing on the forefront of their matching bodies.
I mean—I never felt cold.
My moccasins.
White fur, brown-skinned, flowered dress.
Made for me by my grandpa.
They looked like my gramma.

ZIIBI: White fur, brown-skinned, flowered dress.

MISKOZI: I slipped into their cover.

ZIIBI: White fur.

MISKOZI: And crossed my legs.

ZIIBI: Brown-skinned.

MISKOZI: And sat on the floor.

ZIIBI: Flowered dress.

MISKOZI: And danced.
All in my moccasins.

ZIIBI: White fur, brown-skinned, flowered dress.
(She repeats this under MISKOZI'S text.)

MISKOZI and WAABISHKIZI stop dancing.

MISKOZI: Then
I would—
I would forget about them.
I would take them off.
I would lose them.
(Beat.)
My moccasins...
Whenever I would wear them
It made me
Different.
My moccasins are

MISKOZI &
WAABISHKIZI: Dirty.

MISKOZI: My moccasins are mumbles and stares.
My moccasins are

MISKOZI &
WAABISHKIZI: Dirty.

MISKOZI: My moccasins are an identifier.
My moccasins are...

ZIIBI: White fur, brown-skinned, flowered dress!

    Breath.

Heatstroke

    Transition to Studio 2.

MISKOZI: You know when you're at a wedding... Or a conference... Or like in a real big expensive theatre and there's lots of people and you're looking around and it's like—

> *MISKOZI and WAABISHKIZI look around out at the witnesses.*

Am I... the only... brown person... here?—Oh wait! ...No, nope. Fake tan. Never mind.

> *They both smile and nod and wave politely at all the white people.*
> *WAABISHKIZI begins walking in a spiral.*

MISKOZI: And it's like...
I'm the only one.

But doesn't that make me special?
Like I stand out.
Like I'm important because I stand out.
Right?

> *She looks to WAABISHKIZI.*
> *WAABISHKIZI nods like "Sure!"*

MISKOZI: Right.
And... I don't stand out for the... *wrong* reasons, you know?

> *Beat.*

MISKOZI &
WAABISHKIZI: *(To themselves—thinking out loud.)* What are the wrong reasons?

MISKOZI: What?

WAABISHKIZI: Nothing.

MISKOZI: One time, I saw a guy with a Native Pride hat get shoved down the steps outside the bus depot.
No one helped him.

> *Transition into The Playground.*

> *WAABISHKIZI walks right up to MISKOZI.*

WAABISHKIZI: *(As white person.)* Hey, what's up, token?!

> *They both face forward.*

> *Each section has a gesture.*

MISKOZI &
WAABISHKIZI: Ha ha, token. Yeah—that's funny.

WAABISHKIZI: *(As white person.)* Have you been drinking tonight?

MISKOZI &
WAABISHKIZI: Of course not, officer.

WAABISHKIZI: *(As white person.)* And it was, like, so savage!

MISKOZI &
WAABISHKIZI: Oh yeah—totally.
Savage.

WAABISHKIZI: *(As white person.)* Wow, you're really pretty for a Native.

MISKOZI &
WAABISHKIZI: Oh, um—thank you.

WAABISHKIZI: *(As white person.)* Yo, brown girl!

MISKOZI &
WAABISHKIZI: Ha ha, brown girl. Yeah—that's funny.

WAABISHKIZI: *(As white person.)* Open your bag, please.

MISKOZI &
WAABISHKIZI: Of course, officer.

WAABISHKIZI: *(As white person.)* You look like Pocahontas.

MISKOZI &
WAABISHKIZI: Oh, um—thank you.

WAABISHKIZI: *(As white person.)* I don't see you as an *Indian*,
you know? I see you like as a Native person
because you're not like one of *those* Indians...
like on the street, you know? Like, you're not
like a drunk Indian.
You know?

> *MISKOZI stares straight out — not
> knowing what to say or do.
> WAABISHKIZI steps forward.*

WAABISHKIZI: Yeah.
Yeah, I know.
I totally get it.

> *A long silence.*

> *Something grows.*

MISKOZI: Who doesn't want to feel special, right?
I mean... this is what I wanted.
I surrounded myself in whiteness.
This is what I wanted.
To blend.
To hide.

MISKOZI &
WAABISHKIZI: To mask my face.

WAABISHKIZI: Who doesn't want to feel special?

> *A memory.*

MISKOZI: So I would go out
Out with my white girlfriend
With my white friends
Out
In a field
An event
And the sun

MISKOZI &
WAABISHKIZI: The sun was beating down

MISKOZI: Down
                    On my skin
                    On my head

MISKOZI &
WAABISHKIZI: Beating down
                    Hot
                    On my skin
                    Drinking water

WAABISHKIZI: After bottle

MISKOZI: After water

                    I could feel a twist in my body
                    I turned to my girlfriend
                    My speech was slurring

                    "I'm gonna pass out"

MISKOZI &
WAABISHKIZI: And we're looking for the bus to take us back
                    to the city
                    We're looking for help
                    We're looking for

WAABISHKIZI: *(As The Girlfriend.)* Security!

MISKOZI: Security.

WAABISHKIZI: *(As The Girlfriend.)* We need to get to the bus.

MISKOZI: Security says...

WAABISHKIZI: *(As Security Guard.)* You have to go around.

MISKOZI: But I'm gonna pass out.

WAABISHKIZI: *(As The Girlfriend.)* She has heatstroke!

MISKOZI: But security says...

WAABISHKIZI: *(As Security Guard.)* Tsk! Shouldn't be
                    drinking in this heat.

MISKOZI: I–I haven't been drinking. I'm just... hot.

WAABISHKIZI: *(As Security Guard.)* You have to go around.

MISKOZI: But I'm not drunk.

WAABISHKIZI: *(As Security Guard.)* Shouldn't be drinking in this heat.

MISKOZI: I'm not drunk!

> *MISKOZI gets pulled away by WAABISHKIZI.*

But I'm not drunk!
I'm not drunk!
I'm not drunk!

> *They stop.*
> *WAABISHKIZI holds her hand as they get on the bus.*

MISKOZI: I surrounded myself in whiteness
If I put myself there on purpose
Then at least, I'm laughing at the joke.
I'm not the joke.
Right?
I'm not the joke.
I'm not /

> *A floodlight hits her.*

> Wheel of Fortune *theme song, in vocables.*

> *Transition into Studio 1.*

> *Projection: "Applause"*
> *The audience cheers.*

> *WAABISHKIZI becomes Vanna White.*
> *ZIIBI becomes Pat Sajak.*
> *MISKOZI is confused.*

ZIIBI: *(As Pat Sajak.)* And welcome back! We are still here with... ...our contestant.
                    All right, contestant, what would you like to do?

MISKOZI: I... I don't know anymore...

ZIIBI: *(As Pat Sajak.)* Would you like to spin or solve?

MISKOZI: I just—
                    I don't know if it's worth it anymore. I—

ZIIBI: *(As Pat Sajak.)* Would you like to spin or solve?

MISKOZI: *(Takes a breath—defeated.)* I'll spin.

                            She spins.

                            Projection: "Applause"
                            The audience cheers.

ZIIBI: *(As Pat Sajak.)* Ooh, we have *another* privilege prize if you get this letter. Wowie, they are just handing them out tonight, aren't they?
                    So this is an all-expenses-paid trip to the Isle of Caucasia! Here you will spend a week with a suburban white family where you can brush up on your golf skills, practise drunk yoga and eat bland mashed potatoes.

WAABISHKIZI: *(As Vanna.)* Sounds delicious, Pat.

ZIIBI: *(As Pat Sajak.)* You're from Caucasia, aren't you, Vanna?

WAABISHKIZI: *(As Vanna.)* Well, in the end, don't we all come from Caucasia, Pat?

ZIIBI: *(As Pat Sajak.)* Very true. Very true. Gosh, you're so smart.
                    Isn't she smart, ladies and gentlemen?

Projection: "Applause"
The audience cheers.

ZIIBI: *(As Pat Sajak.)* Smart *and* beautiful. A deadly combination, am I right?

ZIIBI/Pat and WAABISHKIZI/Vanna give an exaggerated laugh.

Projection: "Laugh"
The audience laughs.

ZIIBI: *(As Pat Sajak.)* All right, coming back to the board, what is your guess?

MISKOZI: Uhh.
              "B"?

ZIIBI: *(As Pat Sajak.)* Oooh sorry, no "B"s.
              Well shoot, I guess that means no cold brew at a cottage for you.

Projection: "Boo"
The audience boos.

WAABISHKIZI makes a "darn it" motion with her arm.
MISKOZI looks at WAABISHKIZI.

MISKOZI: I'm so tired.

White Boys Part 2

Transition into Studio 2.

A movement sequence to being hurt and fetishized by more white men.

WAABISHKIZI: *(Whispers and the whisper echoes.)* White boys turn into white men /

MISKOZI: / White boys turn into white men.
                    Turn into white men.

MISKOZI &
WAABISHKIZI: Turn into white men.
                    Turn into…

MISKOZI: White—

MISKOZI &
WAABISHKIZI: One-night, two-night stand-in friends, lovers
                    and companions
                    Tongues lashed out whipping

WAABISHKIZI: Spite

MISKOZI: Tick your box
                    Belt notch
                    This push-up bra is not for you

WAABISHKIZI: But I want you to think it is

MISKOZI: I want you to

MISKOZI &
WAABISHKIZI: Investigate me

WAABISHKIZI: You can't afford it

MISKOZI &
WAABISHKIZI: Comparing our body
                    Comparing our face

WAABISHKIZI: She would be so hot if she were thin

MISKOZI: Had more cream in her coffee

WAABISHKIZI: Stop being so desperate

MISKOZI &
WAABISHKIZI: Comparing our body
                    Comparing our face
                    Such a nice face
                    Such a nice face
                    Such a nice face

WAABISHKIZI: You're not my taste

MISKOZI: But I'm gonna fuck you anyway

>   *Gasp.*

WAABISHKIZI: Look here and smile

MISKOZI: Look here and smile
Smile
Brown
Brown
Browngirl
Token Pocahontas
Tiger Lily slut
Open up your thick legs for anyone looking for a

MISKOZI &
WAABISHKIZI: Good Native fetish

WAABISHKIZI: What are you?

MISKOZI: What are you?

MISKOZI &
WAABISHKIZI: I want your wampum

MISKOZI: Hey ho how hey
Little feather's dizzy from this merry go round

WAABISHKIZI: And around and around and around

MISKOZI: Squaw, bogan, bitch

WAABISHKIZI: You're dangerous

MISKOZI: Drunk, violent, whore

WAABISHKIZI: Indian

MISKOZI: Indian

MISKOZI &
WAABISHKIZI: Deny and ignore

MISKOZI: So I'll cover my face

WAABISHKIZI: War paint

MISKOZI: I'll dye my hair

WAABISHKIZI: War paint

MISKOZI: And I will keep
Playing
Your fucking
Game!

> *Something grows.*

> *ZIIBI flows on, singing.*

ZIIBI: And would sing·
Stories of stars
There is a place long ago...

> *MISKOZI turns away from her.*

> *Transition into The Living Room.*

> *The two girls sit, watching TV.*
> *MISKOZI is visibly upset.*

> *ZIIBI becomes The News.*

ZIIBI: (*As The News.*) This harbour is home to a secret.
It is ripe with human trafficking of First Nations women, young girls and boys who are being lured onto the international ships. Some not making it out alive.

> *A memory.*

MISKOZI: Me and my cousin were just trying to get into the city from the rez...

WAABISHKIZI: "You girls need a ride?" he asked.

MISKOZI: The easiest way is to walk across the bridge.

WAABISHKIZI: No... no, we're fine.

MISKOZI: A truck pulled over alongside us.

WAABISHKIZI: He was white and had a mustache and dark glasses.

MISKOZI: It pretty much cut us off.

WAABISHKIZI: He leaned across and opened the passenger door.

MISKOZI: There were no other people around.

WAABISHKIZI: He patted the seat.

MISKOZI: And we were right next to those docks.

WAABISHKIZI: "Come on. Hop on in," he said.

MISKOZI: No thanks.

WAABISHKIZI: We're just going up the road.

MISKOZI: His tires squealed as he pulled away.

WAABISHKIZI: We were 12 years old.

> Wheel of Fortune *theme song, in vocables.*
>
> *Transition into Studio 1.*
>
> *Projection: "Applause"*
> *The audience cheers.*
>
> *WAABISHKIZI becomes Vanna White.*
> *ZIIBI becomes Pat Sajak.*
> *They smile and wait for MISKOZI to spin.*
> *MISKOZI doesn't. She stays seated.*

ZIIBI: *(As Pat Sajak, still smiling — nothing is wrong.)*
                     What's wrong with her?

WAABISHKIZI: *(As Vanna, also smiling, as if nothing is wrong.)*
                     I haven't the faintest idea, Pat.

ZIIBI: *(As Pat Sajak.)* Well, she had better solve this
                     soon. I have a kara-tay lesson at five.

WAABISHKIZI: *(As Vanna.)* And I'm getting a spray tan.

ZIIBI: *(As Pat Sajak.)* You would think that she
                     would be... a little more grateful.

WAABISHKIZI: *(As Vanna.)* I mean, she's been given the same
                     opportunities as everyone else.

ZIIBI: *(As Pat Sajak.)* More, I would dare say! She
                     doesn't even have to pay taxes.

WAABISHKIZI: *(As Vanna.)* You know what, I'll go talk to her.
                     Woman to woman. We're the same.

                     *WAABISHKIZI/Vanna walks over to her
                     and speaks to her in a Vanna White voice.*

WAABISHKIZI: *(As Vanna.)* Honey! What's wrong?

MISKOZI: I don't want to do this anymore.

WAABISHKIZI: *(As Vanna.)* Well, honey, why not?

MISKOZI: Something doesn't feel right.
                     I don't know if it's worth it.

WAABISHKIZI: *(As Vanna.)* Well. honey, of course it is.
                     Look at all the prizes.
                     The fun, the glamour, the excitement!
                     And you know what's at stake.

MISKOZI: I'm so tired.

WAABISHKIZI: *(As Vanna.)* Honey, we're all tired.

MISKOZI: I don't recognize your face.

WAABISHKIZI: *(As Vanna.)* And honey, you know that it will
                cost you.
                (Beat.)
                It *will* cost you.

MISKOZI: What will it cost me?

WAABISHKIZI: Just a vowel.

> *WAABISHKIZI/Vanna helps her up and
> returns to her post at the board.*
>
> *Projection: "Applause"*
> *The audience cheers.*

MISKOZI: I'd like to buy a vowel.
                "U."

ZIIBI: *(As Pat Sajak.)* One "U"!

> *Projection: "Applause"*
> *The audience cheers.*
> *And cheers.*
> *And cheers.*

Dream—The Trout

> *The In-Between Place.*
>
> *Smoke.*
> *Embers.*
>
> *The two sit, facing each other.*

A small fire between them.
Sparks fly up every so often like sweetgrass
being dragged across a hot stone.
The two mirror each other's movements.
They mime putting on war paint.

The river trickles in.
ZIIBI flows on.

WAABISHKIZI begins to vocalize "There's
a Place."

ZIIBI: *(As the Trout.)* Gda Boonzi naabi epiichi
giizhaa eyaawat-yin
(Gda bohn-zih naah-bih eh-pee-chih gee-
zhaa eh-ya-wot-yin)
Nishke!   **(Nishkay)**

Nishke!
Gshkozi   **(Shkozih)**
Gi-bgizoomgad epiichi biinjii'yii debwewin-
nim
(Gih-bgiz-ohm-gad eh-pee-chih been-jee-
yuh-ee deh-bway-win-im)

MISKOZI: *(Underneath ZIIBI'S text, as if the words are being*
translated through her body.) Stop searching for
what you already have
Look
Look
Open your eyes
You swim in your truth

ZIIBI: *(As the Trout.)* You swim in your truth

MISKOZI: I met a trout fish

ZIIBI: *(As the Trout.)* Why are you crying?

MISKOZI: Who spoke words that were like mist on my
skin

ZIIBI: *(As the Trout.)* You belong

MISKOZI: But it sat there, on my skin

ZIIBI: *(As the Trout.)* It's in your blood

MISKOZI: And I traced lines in it with my fingertips

ZIIBI: *(As the Trout.)* As long as you are of the land

MISKOZI: Trying to understand what they meant

ZIIBI: *(As the Trout.)*Gi-Kaawiikaa gwiinaw
                  (Gih-gaawee-gaa gweena-wey)   *You are*
                  never lost

MISKOZI: They told me a story about a little girl
                  Playing in a forest near the river
                  Throwing stones
                  Admiring the ripples
                  Trying to chase her reflection
                  When the floods came
                  The waters of the river swallowed her up
                  Turned her inside out
                  She felt her bones twist
                  Her blood became sand
                  When she came out the other side
                  She expected to be different
                  She expected to be changed
                  But when she looked in the river
                  Her reflection remained the same

MISKOZI &
WAABISHKIZI: You swim in your truth

WAABISHKIZI: But our lips remained dry

MISKOZI: They swam away
                  With a trail of sage
                  And turtle tears
                  That looked so much like my own

                  The river rushes in.
                  Submersion.

The fire goes out.

The wind begins to blow.

Plastic Sandals

Transition into The Living Room.

MISKOZI paces, agitated.
WAABISHKIZI does the same thing,
opposite direction.

MISKOZI: Okay. Okay.
Umm—oh! The internet! The internet has answers, right?
It has all the answers.

WAABISHKIZI sits at a computer and begins to type.
MISKOZI leans over her.

MISKOZI: Let's see... okay, umm...

WAABISHKIZI: Oh look, there's gonna be a powwow!
Remember when we went to powwows?

MISKOZI: ...Yeah... sort of.
We were really young.

WAABISHKIZI: I liked the colours.

Beat.

Love

MISKOZI: Me too.

WAABISHKIZI: We should go to this one!

MISKOZI: ...Yeah, maybe.

I don't know, though. Shouldn't I, like...
know... more... first?

WAABISHKIZI: Hmm. Maybe you're right.
What should we look up?

MISKOZI: I'm not sure. I don't know where to start
looking.
I mean... Pocahontas at least had help from a
tree... and that raccoon.

WAABISHKIZI: Meeko.

MISKOZI: Right. Meeko. So... maybe we need /

WAABISHKIZI: / Ooh! I got it.

She types.

WAABISHKIZI: "What is my spirit animal?"

MISKOZI: Oh, there's a quiz.
Okay /

WAABISHKIZI: / Mine is totally Jennifer Lawrence.

MISKOZI looks at her.

WAABISHKIZI: She's just SO relatable, you know?

MISKOZI: Okay. What's the first question?

WAABISHKIZI: What hairstyle suits you best?
The Rachel.
The Farrah.
The Cher.
Or The Wednesday Adams.

MISKOZI: Uhh— *(She touches her hair, insecure.)* The...
Cher? I... guess?

WAABISHKIZI: Makes sense.
Cherokee princess.

All right.
Question 2.

Which shade is your foundation?

Chocolate cherry.
Caramel drizzle.
Graham cracker crumble.
Or vanilla sunshine sparkle princess.

MISKOZI: I'm not a friggin' ice cream sundae!

WAABISHKIZI: I mean—graham cracker crumble does sound delicious.

MISKOZI: Okay... I guess I'll go with that one?

WAABISHKIZI: Good choice.
                       Next—

                       What is your sense of style?

                       Boho chic.
                       Hippie happy.
                       Easy breezy.
                       Or free and open.

MISKOZI: Those... all sound the same.

WAABISHKIZI: Oh, they're very different, look.
                       That girl is wearing a blue scarf.
                       But this one is yellow.
                       See?

MISKOZI: What kind of quiz is this??

WAABISHKIZI: It's certified!

MISKOZI: By who??

WAABISHKIZI: Ummm…Girlbosswellness.org

MISKOZI: *(Sighs.)* What's the next question?

WAABISHKIZI: Okay. Final one.
               What was the last song you heard in your dreams?

MISKOZI: What?

WAABISHKIZI: I said, what song would you play to go to sleep?

MISKOZI: That's... not....

WAABISHKIZI: "Sweet Dreams" by The Eurythmics.
               "Daydream Believer" by The Monkees.
               "Dreams" by Fleetwood Mac.
               Or "Teenage Dream" by Katy Perry?

MISKOZI: I... which one would you pick?

               She smiles.
               WAABISHKIZI starts singing "Dreams"
               by Fleetwood Mac.
               After a beat, MISKOZI joins in.
               WAABISHKIZI really gets into it. She gets
               to the fourth line when…

               MISKOZI sees the results of the quiz.

MISKOZI: What the fuck is Sheebu Eenu?
               Is that a dog?

WAABISHKIZI: *(Reads from the screen.)* Oh! You got: Shiba Inu.
               You're very curious about the way things
               work, but that doesn't mean you don't have a
               smile on everywhere you go. You're friendly,
               loyal, and you have a certain fondness for
               misspellings!

MISKOZI: What?

WAABISHKIZI: *(Seriously.)* This is what our ancestors wanted.

MISKOZI: This is—this can't be right.

WAABISHKIZI: Well, how do we know what's right?

MISKOZI: I don't know!
I don't know anything.
I don't *have* anyone to tell me!
We're all confused!
I can't even ask Grandma and Grandpa any questions
Because they're gone.
Like what am I supposed to do?
Google how to be a Native?
What am I even doing?
Maybe I shouldn't have moved off the rez.
But would staying have made a difference?
Ugh, this is so / frustrating...

WAABISHKIZI: / For a person to be considered Native by the government, they must either have a CDIB card—certificate of degree of Indian blood—or be enrolled in a tribe.

MISKOZI: What are you talking about?

WAABISHKIZI: I Googled how to be a Native.

Deep sigh.

Transition into Studio 2.

MISKOZI: Someone at work asked me today.

WAABISHKIZI: *(As colleague.)* Oh my GOD, are *you* Native?!

MISKOZI and WAABISHKIZI stare at each other.

A moment.

WAABISHKIZI faces forward.

WAABISHKIZI: Umm...

Something grows.

MISKOZI: I didn't know what to say. I mean I am.
I am.

But I could have said any ethnicity with brown skin and she would have been like /

WAABISHKIZI: (*As colleague.*) / Woooooooooooow

MISKOZI:
I am.
But I didn't want...
I just feel like—
Like if I said it, I would feel like a fraud.
You know?
Like when I say it, it feels like I'm wearing some sort of mask.
Like I'm in red face.
It's like these layers.
I'm red.
I'm smudged.
I'm smeared.
I'm tossed.
I'm turned.

MISKOZI &
WAABISHKZI:
I'm white.
I'm white.
I'm white.

MISKOZI:
I'm exotic.
I'm—
What am I?
I'm red?
I'm red.
I'm red!

I *feel* like a fraud though.
Like I'm—like I'm a white girl.

Like I convinced myself so hard that I'm a white girl
that I let *everyone* convince me that I'm a white girl.
But I look down at my feet and I see that...
that it's like I'm still wearing my moccasins, you know?

And that, like, that pisses me off, you know?
Like I was always bothered whenever I saw a
white girl wearing moccasins, you know?
Like something deep, deep down inside of
me hated seeing it.
And when I'm white, I—

MISKOZI &
WAABISHKIZI: I don't know why it bothers me so much.

MISKOZI: But when I'm red, I'm like...
Hey—where'd you get those moccasins
from?
Did you buy them at the mall?
Did you buy them at the mall?
Alongside cheap plastic sandals?
Rubber bracelets and rings made of fucking
fake diamond bows or whatever?

WAABISHKIZI: Did you buy those moccasins from next to a
box of brightly-coloured nail polishes?
From a store next to a fucking Starbucks?
With a bunch of "aboriginal stuff"?
Fake dreamcatchers and headdress costumes.

The wind picks up.

MISKOZI: Do you wear my face when you drink your
booze?
When you tan your skin golden to look like
mine?
Where did you buy those moccasins from,
white girl?
Was it from my cousin?
With her painstaking beading?
Her personal patterns?
Or from Shelly down the road?
Who sells them at the fairs?
Or from my grandpa?
Did you buy them from my grandpa!?

Who worked every night in his trailer,
Building,
Making,
Crafting,
Just to survive?!

A realization.

My moccasins are survival.
My moccasins are stories.
My moccasins are not your next cool trend.
My moccasins are...

> *The river rushes in around them.*
> *ZIIBI flows on.*

ZIIBI: White fur, brown-skinned, flowered dress.

> *MISKOZI looks at her for the first time...*
> *in a long time.*

MISKOZI: I know your face.

> *ZIIBI begins to sing the vocables from*
> *"There's a Place."*

ZIIBI: WEY YA HEY YAA WEY HEY YA WEY YA
AH ...

> *MISKOZI begins to sing with her, then*
> *stops herself.*

ZIIBI &
MISKOZI: WEY YA HEY YAA WEY HEY YA /....

MISKOZI: / I feel so stupid.

> *The wind blows harder.*

The Blizzard

Projection: The game board appears.

ZIIBI: Maybe you should buy a vowel

MISKOZI: How will that help me?

ZIIBI: There's something that you need to find.

MISKOZI stands back and looks at the board.

MISKOZI: I'd like to buy an "E."

ZIIBI: There are three "E"s.

WAABISHKIZI turns the letters.

MISKOZI takes in the puzzle, her body reacts to it.

Heavy breath.

The wind blows even harder.

ZIIBI begins to beat the hand drum.

The drum beats faster and faster.

*There is
A wakening.
A reclamation.
A knowing.
A truth.*

A different kind of storm.

It begins to snow in the studios and in The Living Room and on The Playground, covering everything in white.
The projection turns to blowing snow.

A blizzard.
MISKOZI is submerged in it.

MISKOZI begins to repeat the lost movement sequence but pulls roots out of her body instead.

WAABISHKIZI yells over the storm.

WAABISHKIZI: Tell me how we got here!

MISKOZI: I feel like I've lost something and I don't know what it is.
There's something missing!

WAABISHKIZI: Tell me where it began!

Breath.

Suddenly everything stops.

Suspension.

MISKOZI: I... was gonna apply for a new job.
And it's for an Indigenous company, so I don't know if I... should because I'm scared that I need to know all of the cultural things that I'm supposed to know.
I should know them.
But I don't.
So I went to see a healer first and they invited me to go to a sweat because I was confused. I was scared. But they–they spoke words that were like mist on my skin...

Transition to The Sweat Lodge.

Smoke.

Embers.
Sparks.

ZIIBI as the Healer begins moving the stones.

ZIIBI: *(As the Healer/Trout.)*
Boozhoo Nishoomis
(Boo-zhoo Ni-shoh-mis)   W e l c o m e
Grandfather
Boozhoo Nookomis
(Boo-zhoo Noh-koh-mis)   W e l c o m e
Grandmother

MISKOZI: They said that there was something that I needed to find.

ZIIBI: *(As the Healer/Trout.)*
Boozhoo Nishoomis   **(Boo-zhoo Ni-shoh-mis)**
Boozhoo Nookomis   **(Boo-zhoo Noh-koh-mis)**

MISKOZI: They said that I needed to look back to go forward.

ZIIBI: *(As the Healer/Trout.)*
Boozhoo Nishoomis   **(Boo-zhoo Ni-shoh-mis)**
Boozhoo Nookomis   **(Boo-zhoo Noh-koh-mis)**

MISKOZI: They said that I needed to listen for my ancestors and that all of us, no matter where we are in our journey—

MISKOZI
& ZIIBI   *(As the Healer/Trout):*
All of us are sacred.

ZIIBI: *(As the Healer/Trout.)* And are deserving of ceremony.

ZIIBI/The Healer gestures for her to help.
The two begin to move the rocks together.

MISKOZI
& ZIIBI

(as the Healer/Trout):
Boozhoo Nishoomis   **(Boo-zhoo Ni-shoh-mis)**

Boozhoo Nookomis   **(Boo-zhoo Noh-koh-mis)**

Darkness.

Breath.

Sparks.

Remember (BIINJIIY'II GI-MSKWII-M) (reprise)

ZIIBI/Healer begins to sing.
The song is slower.
As she sings, more and more ancestral voices join her.
Sparks fly all around them.
Ancestors make their presence known.

ZIIBI:

(As the Healer/Trout.)   BIINJIIY'II GI
(been-jee-yuh-ee gih)
BIINJIIY'II GI
BIINJIIY'II GI
MSKWII-M   **(miss-gwee'm)**

BIINJIIY'II GI
BIINJIIY'II GI

BIINJIIY'II GI
MSKWII-M

GI-KAAWIIKAA   **(Gih-gaa-wee-gaa)**
GI-KAAWIIKAA
GI-KAAWIIKAA

GWIINAW WAY HEY YO **(gweenaw)**

GI-KAAWIIKAA
GI-KAAWIIKAA
GI-KAAWIIKAA
GWIINAW WAY HEY YO

GWIINAW WAY HEY YO
GWIINAW WAY HEY YO

> *The suspension drops out.*
> *The wind returns.*

> *MISKOZI stands.*

MISKOZI: My feet are cold.

ZIIBI: White fur.
Brown-skinned.
Flowered dress.

MISKOZI: I know your face.

ZIIBI: And I know yours.

MISKOZI: What do I do?

ZIIBI: There's something you need to find.

> *MISKOZI turns to a pile of snow.*
> *She begins to dig.*
> *And eventually, pulls out her moccasins.*
> *She dusts them off.*
> *She stares at them.*

> *The wind calms.*

> *MISKOZI puts the moccasins on her feet.*

MISKOZI: It feels like I've finally caught my breath.

MISKOZI &
WAABISHKIZI: I didn't realize I wasn't breathing.

MISKOZI: I didn't know I was holding my breath.

WAABISHKIZI: I didn't realize.

MISKOZI: I was holding on to so much.
                      So much that

MISKOZI &
WAABISHKIZI: Wasn't mine to hold.

> *Beat.*
>
> *A realization.*

MISKOZI: This isn't my fault.

> *She looks at her skin.*

"You be proud of your skin, my girl."

> *She touches her skin.*

Be proud.

> *And touches her skin.*
> *And continues to touch and fall in love with*
> *her skin.*

Brown is like
Brown is like the earth
Where food and flowers grow
Brown is like the soft hair on the animals that
we love
Brown is like shades of night under full
moons
Outlines
Solid
And dark
The darkness is what holds us
And keeps us

Brown is like silk
Like satin that wraps around us and sinks
into our pores
It's beautiful.
I'm beautiful.

It isn't my fault that whiteness was my base
That sometimes I saw a white girl staring
through my face
It isn't my fault that I needed her to survive
That she kept me safe
It isn't my fault that I have so much work to
do
To learn
And unlearn
And relearn
And reclaim
Joys and teachings that were taken away
Stolen away
Hidden in places we'd never look to find
Inside our bodies
Inside our minds
And we grabbed what we could
But it isn't my fault that our arms weren't big
enough to hold everything

It isn't
Our
Fault

And what do you do
Once you've opened your eyes
Because I can't close mine now
Can you?

The last of the snow falls.

The Puzzle

Projection: The game board appears.

MISKOZI: I'd like to solve.

Gi-Kaawiikaa gwiinaw
(Gih-gaa-wee-gaa gween-awey)

The puzzle fills in.

Something else grows—blooms and connects.
A circle.
A oneness.

Stars.

Breath.

The river rushes.

MISKOZI: Biinjiiy'ii g-mskwii-m
(been-jee-yuh-ee guh-miss-gwee'm)

ZIIBI: In your blood

MISKOZI: Nji-aki-ing maajiishka
(Njih akeh-ing ma-jeesh-gaa)

ZIIBI: Of the land

MISKOZI: You are never lost

There is a Place (reprise)

> *ZIIBI begins to sing.*

> *ZIIBI and MISKOZI move in a way together like they would have a very long time ago.*

ZIIBI: THERE IS A PLACE
WHERE HEALING BEGINS
AND ANCESTORS WHISPER IN MY DREAMS

> *ZIIBI begins to drum.*

> *As MISKOZI sings with ZIIBI, her and WAABISHKIZI begin moving as one. MISKOZI is reconciling with WAABISHKIZI.*
> *Beginning to heal.*

ZIIBI &
MISKOZI: LIKE THE WIND
LIKE WATER RIPPLING
THERE IS A PLACE WHERE I HAVE BEEN
MY SOUL IT SINGS STORIES OF SCARS
MY SOUL IT SINGS STORIES OF SCARS

ZIIBI: THERE IS A PLACE WHERE HEALING BEGINS
SWIMMING TOGETHER IN MY BLOOD

MISKOZI: I WILL REMEMBER IT'S IN MY BLOOD

> *Four drumbeats.*

> *Darkness.*

> *Stars.*

Supplemental Material

Director's Notes
from the world premiere of White Girls in Moccasins, 2022

White Girls in Moccasins by Yolanda Bonnell is in an ongoing conversation with celebrated and celestial works such as the late 2 Spirit playwright Daniel David Moses (Haudenosaunee) whose play *Almighty Voice and His Wife* (1992) features a two-act structure, the first dramatizing a historical event and the second leaning into the abstract to highlight the personal impacts of colonialism.

There are resonances with *Salt Baby* (2009) by Falen Johnson (Mohawk-Tuscarora), a comedy that shines bright with humour, nostalgia, and a heartfelt search for oneself within family and community.

And it sits beyond the stratosphere among powerful creator/ performers like the Turtle Gals Performance Ensemble (Jani Lauzon, Monique Mojica and Michelle St. John) whose play *The Scrubbing Project* (2002) brings ceremony, in the form of a ritual feast, to an exploration of genocide and difficult truths that continue to be overcome by Indigenous peoples today.

The coproduction stewarded by the leadership at Buddies, the lessons we're learning at manidoons, the vitality of Indigenous, Black, and culturally diverse folx and our ability to laugh, and love, and heal.

We are a circle of artists bringing ourselves to this work and we invite you to join us out here among the stars.

—Cole Alvis

***

Where to start... My journey with *White Girls in Moccasins* began as a workshop; after the first read-through I immediately knew this story needed to be told.

I saw myself in this story and I knew many others would too. Yolanda has a way of writing that challenges societal issues on a broad scale while maintaining a story that is deeply personal and intimate. The poetry of the text is so moving and layered but also incredibly witty and hilarious. This journey begins on the page with rich text but becomes an act of artistic ceremony in the storytelling. This artistic ceremony is unlike anything I've witnessed or been a part of before. The amount of care and deep listening that is embedded in the process is a radical challenge to the way theatre across Turtle Island has previously been conducted. This is a healing journey for each character, and also an active offer of how to begin a healing practice within the theatre industry. I am so grateful to be a member in this circle and I have learned so much from the witnessing of this offering. We actively heal our ancestors when we live our truth out loud; this artistic ceremony is an invitation towards that healing.

—Samantha Brown

Anishinaabemowin
By Yolanda Bonnell

I was never taught my traditional language. I remember hearing my grandmother speak it on the phone to her sister, but she wouldn't teach it to us. The shame that colonization and assimilation brought to us created the idea that we just had no use for it anymore—at least on my reservation. I know there are some communities that were able to retain language keepers that could continue to produce fluent speakers, but they still really did a number on our mother tongues across the board.

They tried to take it completely away from us. You can see it in the residential schools, the creation of reservations, the laws that were put in place that made it illegal for us to practise our ceremonies and speak Anishinaabemowin to each other.

They tried.

But so many of our ancestors were resilient and they held onto words, phrases, songs, stories. They held on tight while that apocalyptic storm of colonization ripped right through us.

Growing up, I remember hearing the difference in how my family spoke. The way some spoke English wasn't always the way I was being taught in school.

I had a natural gift of creation and wanted to be a writer/storyteller from a young age. I read as much as I could and wrote down words I didn't understand to look up later in the dictionary. It made me feel important to feel smart. To feel like I was doing well in school—particularly in English. It became clear to me what was viewed as *well-spoken* or *grammatically correct* wasn't what I was growing up around. My mother would say certain words *incorrectly*, others would say sentences where words were put in the I *wrong* order grammatically, some words weren't in sentences at all, oftentimes there was no *h* in words with *th*, and there was barely a *g* to be found at the end of words ending in *ing*. Slap a thick rez accent on there with some Nishnawb slang and expressions and it's a whole other world of slights against the Queen's English. Oh my!

So... I learned how to code switch as quickly as possible and worked really hard to be the best speller and writer. And I'm sure living on and off the rez sporadically helped me in that learning.

It took me far too long to realize that what I was hearing and critiquing around me was a version of broken English. They—Canada, the church and the Crown—made us speak their language but didn't take the time to teach most people *properly* because what's an Indian gonna do in the real world anyway, right? They just needed to be able to communicate with people and they needed to know that there was an understanding when Indians were being put in their place. No need to have grammatically correct sentences for that. From what I understand, there *were* groups of Indigenous kids who went through a type of etiquette and domestic *training* mostly through residential schools. The colonial forces did invest in the smarter ones, the quiet ones, their favourites, and pushed them further to succeed as Canada formed the exotic idea of the noble savage; the only

Indian they would accept in society.

I felt a lot of shame when all of this hit me. I spent so much time correcting and judging—especially myself and it made me feel like they won, you know? This is what Canada wanted. A well-spoken Indian. And a well-spoken Indian can go far in this newer world. I had no strong trace of my traditional language—except for some slang words and *miigwetch*. I didn't have any access to Ojibwe-Anishinaabe practices—except for powwow. No real medicine teachings. All land teachings were done in almost a code—they were done in the *doing*; not spoken out loud and I have the ability to speak like a customer service white lady, very well. On paper, it sounds like they did, in fact, *kill the Indian in the child.*

But, as we know (or should know), they didn't. That's not what happened.

I just had to unearth a few things to find my way back home. The Indian was always there and never left. Just as it never left my grandmother or her mother and father or their parents.

I've done a lot of work to rid myself of that shame and de-colonize the way I speak English. (Also—criticizing the way anyone speaks English can be classist and is often racist, so let's all maybe stop doing that.) I am still proud of myself for my achievements and proud that I am where I am. And I hope that I would be just as proud if I wasn't. I mean, it's complicated. I think it's complicated for a lot of us. And I tried to put all of that complication in this story.

I think writing this play was a part of undoing the shame and working to reclaim. To understand that it wasn't my fault. It's not any of our faults. When you're whitewashed and indoctrinated into a colonial world that you have to navigate, you do what you can to keep your head up and above water. We did what our ancestors have always done: survive.

I've been trying to teach myself Anishinaabemowin for the last seven years. Not in depth enough, but through as many resources as I can find. And yes, some of them are from the internet because there are some good things there! When I first wrote the script, I had to cobble together what I could to translate the sections I wanted. They were the crudest of translations and probably made very little sense, but the point was that I was trying. It can be difficult to reclaim a language that's also been colonized in a way. Navigating dialects—north, south, east, west—some that vary community to community. Trying to find my own inside it all.

I eventually hired language keepers for the piece, but I think it was important for me to try on my own first. As the wonderful Leslie McCue says: I speak the language because it makes my ancestors happy.

You can see my trying in this text. I think there's a part of me that wanted the whole Prologue scene to be in Anishinaabemowin up until the point where contact happens. But I feel that would be antithetical to my actual experience with language and why and how I wrote this piece. The words in the opening sit between English and broken Anishinaabemowin for a reason. That the sense of the entire story lives in the actual creation of the text itself.

I hope I am making my ancestors happy. By documenting. The Ojibwe were named the scroll keepers when the Three Fires Confederacy was formed. This might not be made out of wigwas (birchbark) but it is a print.

I would say that this is the documented attempt at language reclamation by a generational survivor of the great apocalypse of colonial occupation on Turtle Island.

And I will keep on attempting.

Here is a list of the Anishinaabemowin names, words, phrases that appear in the story.

Names

These are the only translations I did that remained.

MISKOZI   (Mis-koh-zih)   she is red

WAABISHKIZI   (Waa-bish-kih-zih)   she is white
ZIIBI   (Zee-bih)   river

Ziibi's Messages

Ziibi continues to try and communicate with Miskozi throughout the piece, but particularly through her dreams. The overall answer to Miskozi's search for her missing cultural identity—that question of: *Am I Native enough?* Being: it's in your blood and as long as you remember that you are from the land, you are never lost. Ziibi is trying to tell her that her cultural identity has been within her the entire time.

Biinjiiy'ii gi-mskwii-m   (Been-jee-yuh-ee gih-miss-gwee'm)
In your blood

Nji-aki-ing maajiishka   (Njih akih-ing ma-jeesh-guh)
From the earth

Gi-Kaawiikaa gwiinaw   (Gih-gaa-wee-gaa gween-awey)
You are never lost (uncertain / restless)

Gda Boonzi naabi epiichi giizhaa eyaawat-yin
(Gda bohn-zih naah-bih eh-pee-chay gee-zhaa eh-ya-wot-yin)

Stop searching for what you already have

Nishke!   (Nishkay)   Look!
Gshkozi   (Shkozih)   Open your eyes

Gi-bgizoomgad epiichi biinjii'yii debwewin-nim
(Gih-bgiz-ohm-gad eh-pee-chih been-jee-yuh-ee deh-bway-win-im)
You swim in your truth

Debwewin   (deh-bway-win)   Truth

Miskozi Hears

Miskozi begins to hear and understand more and more in her dreams to the point where the language slips through her as well. She even begins to translate what Ziibi is saying to her.

Nshkiizhigoo   (Nish-gee-zhih-go)   My eyes

Ni-deh-em   (Neh-deh-em)   My heart

"Ni deh em" is also the name of a song Ziibi sings while Miskozi and Waabishkizi are trying to heal themselves.

The Healer

Ziibi transforms into numerous different entities throughout to get Miskozi's attention, but often returns to the trout fish or healer. The healer appearing as a trout fish is meant to symbolize healing through the land—again bringing back that idea that that's where Miskozi's answers are. Land=body. Body=land.

When we are transported back to the sweat lodge, Ziibi takes on the form of the healer or conductor of the ceremony and welcomes the rocks (our grandparents) into the space. It's here where the catalyst of the story exists as the healer is the one that told Miskozi that she must look back to go forward. By looking back to where it all began (first contact/colonization) through to her own beginnings, Miskozi is able to finally find the answers.

Boozhoo Nishoomis   (Boo-zhoo Ni-shoh-mis)   Welcome
Grandfather
Boozhoo Nookomis   (Boo-zhoo Noh-koh-mis)   Welcome
Grandmother

GI-KAAWIIKAA GWIINAW
YOU ARE NEVER LOST

A Poem

When I first started creating this story, I wrote a poem/spoken word piece that was a part of the script. At first it made up the ending and then it was split into the opening and ending and then moved back to the end again, but cut shorter.

It was a poem that I wrote as a response to what I had begun to learn and realize about the truth of my own colonial history and the history of Canada and Indigenous peoples. It was my anger and rage at finally understanding where a lot of my trauma and my family's trauma had seeded from. It was my eyes finally opening. And it had its time and place in the piece, but it never seemed to *fit* properly.

I came to find that it wasn't anger that the ending needed—it was healing. The anger is there. It's already there. It brought Miskozi to the place where she needed to be. I had a duty to start her on the healing path.

But I needed this poem to get to the ending that the story has now. So I share it here because it too, deserves to be recognized, as all of our anger and rage does.

A content warning: the entire poem speaks to the horrible traumas and violence that have been inflicted upon Indigenous people since colonization and continue to be. Some words and phrases might be difficult to read.

Sigh, Spit & Dance

Where are the lines drawn between you and me?
My eyes are wide open but I still can't seem to see
The sharp edges and the textures of my broken-down skin
Cell to cell
Head to toe
All my in-betweens
Slathered in melanin
I let the oceans in
Those ones I've never seen
I scream and I scream and still no relief
Tell me what am I supposed to do with this information?
These restrictions placed upon me
This sin
This sin has no context or relation
And my sisters
My sisters
That have no eyes to see
My sisters that are dying out in the motherfucking streets
And in ditches
And in doorways

And in rivers; lakes and streams
Their ever-precious bodies lie with no resolution or relief
And the grief
The grief is so large it eats my people up
Covered in their tears, past the point of love
As our leaders and this country turn their heads aside
While our still forgotten youth are taking their own lives
Can you drink from your tap?
Dip a toe into your river?
Do you have to pay higher costs for a litre?
"Fix the Indian problem"
Eradicate
Exterminate
Negotiate?
No
You think they'll let us flow?
We live with awareness that this genocide is slow
Go Go Go
You call us drunken Natives, beggars
Hard to handle
First you make the alcoholic
Then you punish for the bottle?
Our elders are in agony
Refuse to speak the language
Hide inside their rooms, whispers, trying to forget
The memories
The tortures
Their brains are at a duel
Trying to erase the horrors of the residential schools
Our braids got cut
Souls got cut
Mouth sewn shut
Raped and pushed aside
Beaten with hands that should have held us while we cried
Here come the black robes
Here come the church
Here come your white God
White God forgive our souls
Our beliefs are of the Devil
Our spirit wrong

Taught us all your songs
Assimilate. Conform.
Conform or die
The trick is we'll die anyway
You just don't know where or why
It could be on a farm in Saskatoon like Colten Boushie
And yet, gun in hand that white man got a not guilty
You shoved us onto reservations, made us form the band
And yet you run those pipelines directly through our lands
I shout into the void where my culture used to last
I pass by my past
My accent didn't last
This line didn't cast
My breath is running fast
Gasp gasp
Sigh, spit and dance
The drumming feeds my soul
Look at me!
Look at me!
Tell me
Did I say something, anything you didn't know?
Did I?
Tell me, where are the lines drawn between you and me?
I'm so smothered in your culture
My own, I can barely see